The Sound of Silence

A Journey of Recovery

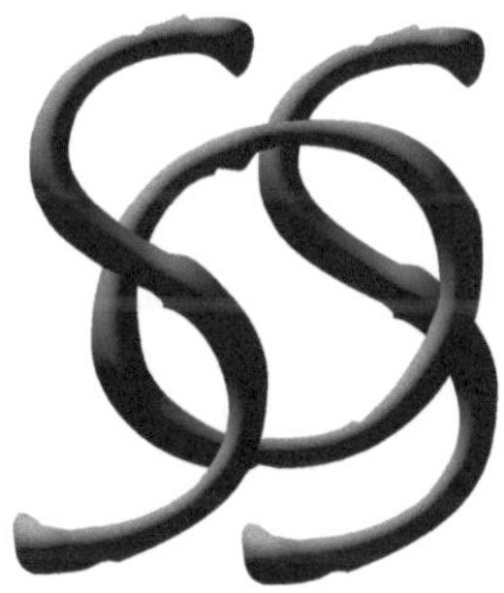

Fred A. Hunt

Hays, Kansas
Another24.org Book

The images in this book are available as fine art prints and mixed media art at
www.fredhuntphotography.com

The Sound of Silence: A Journey of Recovery

First Printing, 2012

ISBN: 978-0-9859939-0-0
Library of Congress Control Number: 2012914211

An Another24.org Book
Editors Melissa Stramel and Fred Hunt

Dedicated to my brothers... lost too soon and to everyone who still struggles.

In loving memory of:

Matt Pfannenstiel
Feb. 3, 2011
Age 33

Jeff Martin
June 24, 2011
Age 34

Don't get too crazy up there guys. Leave some fun for the rest of us when we get there!

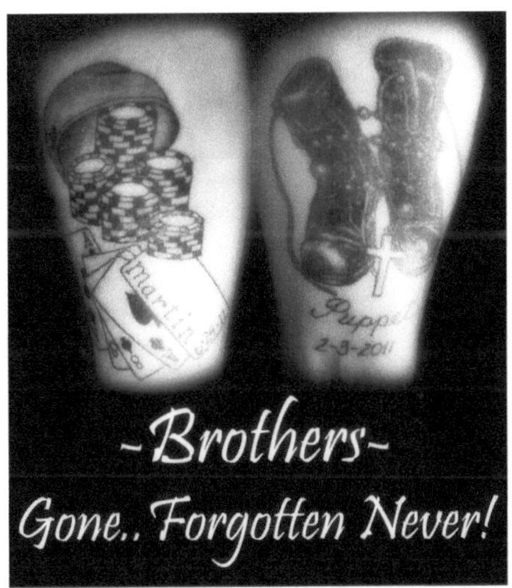

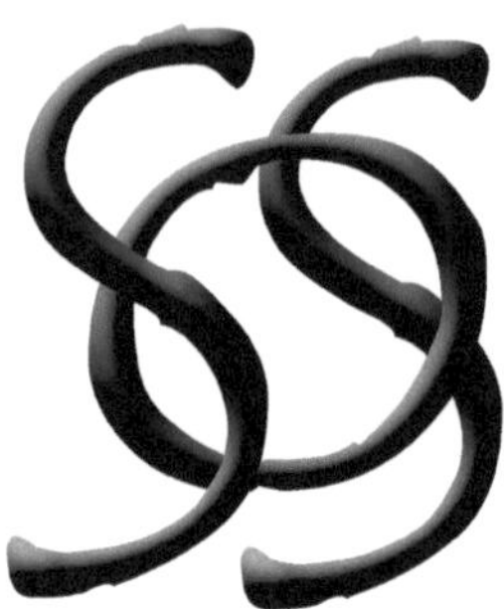

In 2010, I had given up being a photographer. Writing and creating art were painful memories, belonging to someone I thought I'd lost forever.

On October 31, 2010, I sought help at Valley Hope Treatment Center, and it saved my life. In the seven months that followed, I took the trip covered in this book, and lost two close friends to the disease of alcoholism.

If you or someone you know is suffering from alcoholism, please get help before it is too late. . A new life is possible but it can't be done alone.

A portion of the proceeds are given to the Valley Hope Foundation and their fight to save lives.

(This book is in no way connected to, supported by, or endorsed by the Valley Hope Foundation.)

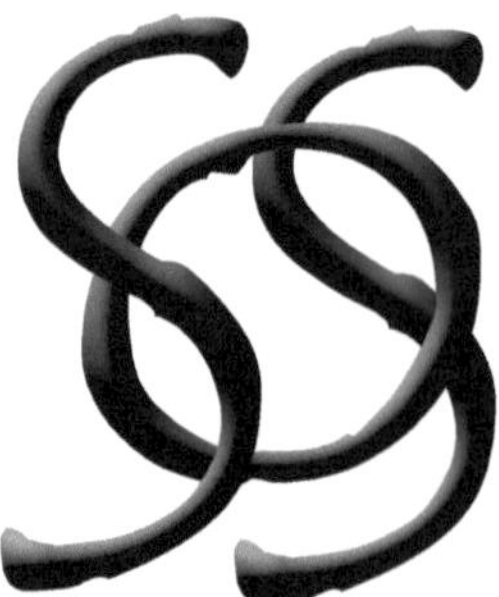

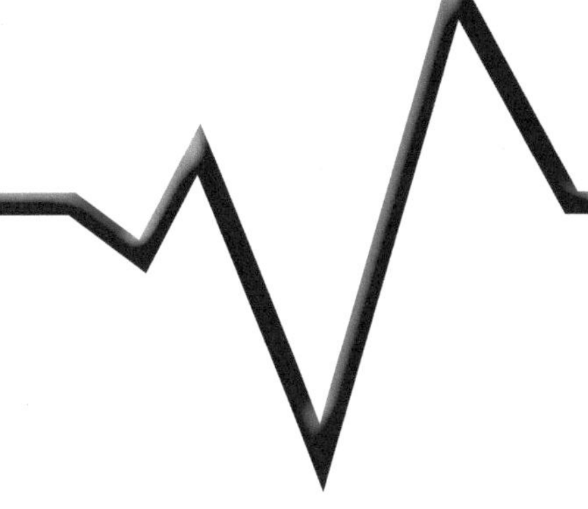

Expressions of Thanks

Special thanks to Nex-Tech and Pete Felten for the use of their galleries. To Chris at Casual Graphics for his amazing print quality and ideas. To Ft. Hays State University's Leland Powers for the suggestion, and Linda Gangstrom for making me feel like an artist again. And to my brother, Randy and his wife Kim, without whom I never would have seen the doors of hope. Thanks to Cyndi Danner-Kuhn for opening the world of photography to me and to my Aunt Edna who made this book a reality.

Thanks to Kim for the delicious food and ideas through good times and bad. To Dan, for being there when I really needed someone and for your tolerance when I could not even see the cards. You saved my life, my Friend.

To Pam- you are a saint and treasured as such. Once again, I couldn't have done this without you.

To Melissa- thank you for the faith you have in me, for calming my doubts and inspiring me when I'm stuck. You bring hope, meaning and depth to my life as only you could. Remember, there is no such place as far away, when you love someone.

To all the workers & staff at Norton Valley Hope: None of this would have happened without your compassionate and caring work.

Most importantly, thank you, Mom for never giving up on me!

Sound Of Silence

It is the sound you can only hear in the isolated places of the world. Mountain tops, oceans, deserts, places where, surrounded by vast emptiness, you become part of everything and everything becomes part of you. It is in the void of silence that you hear the heartbeat of the world.

Great Sand Dunes National Park and Preserve

Southeastern Colorado

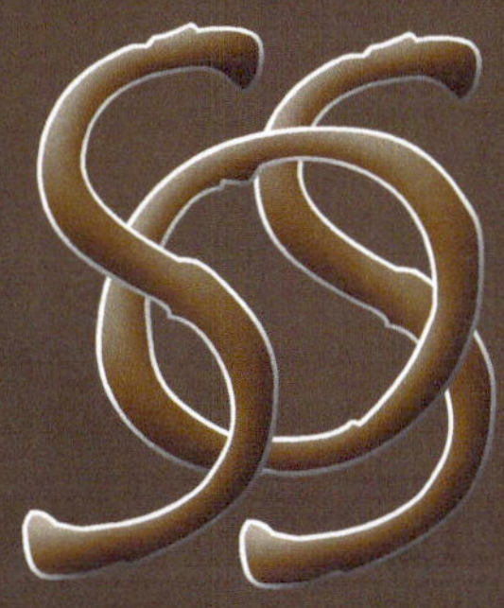

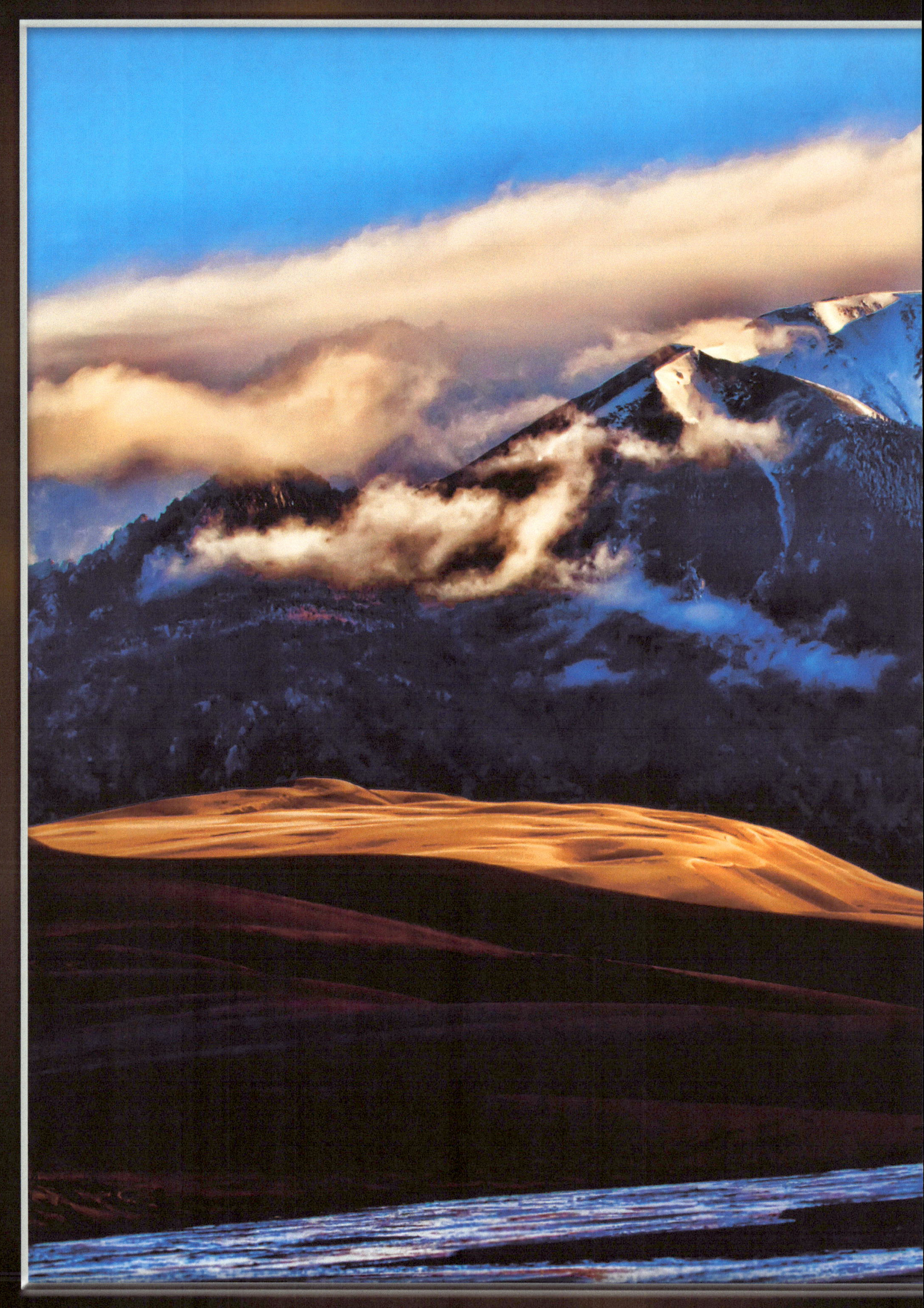

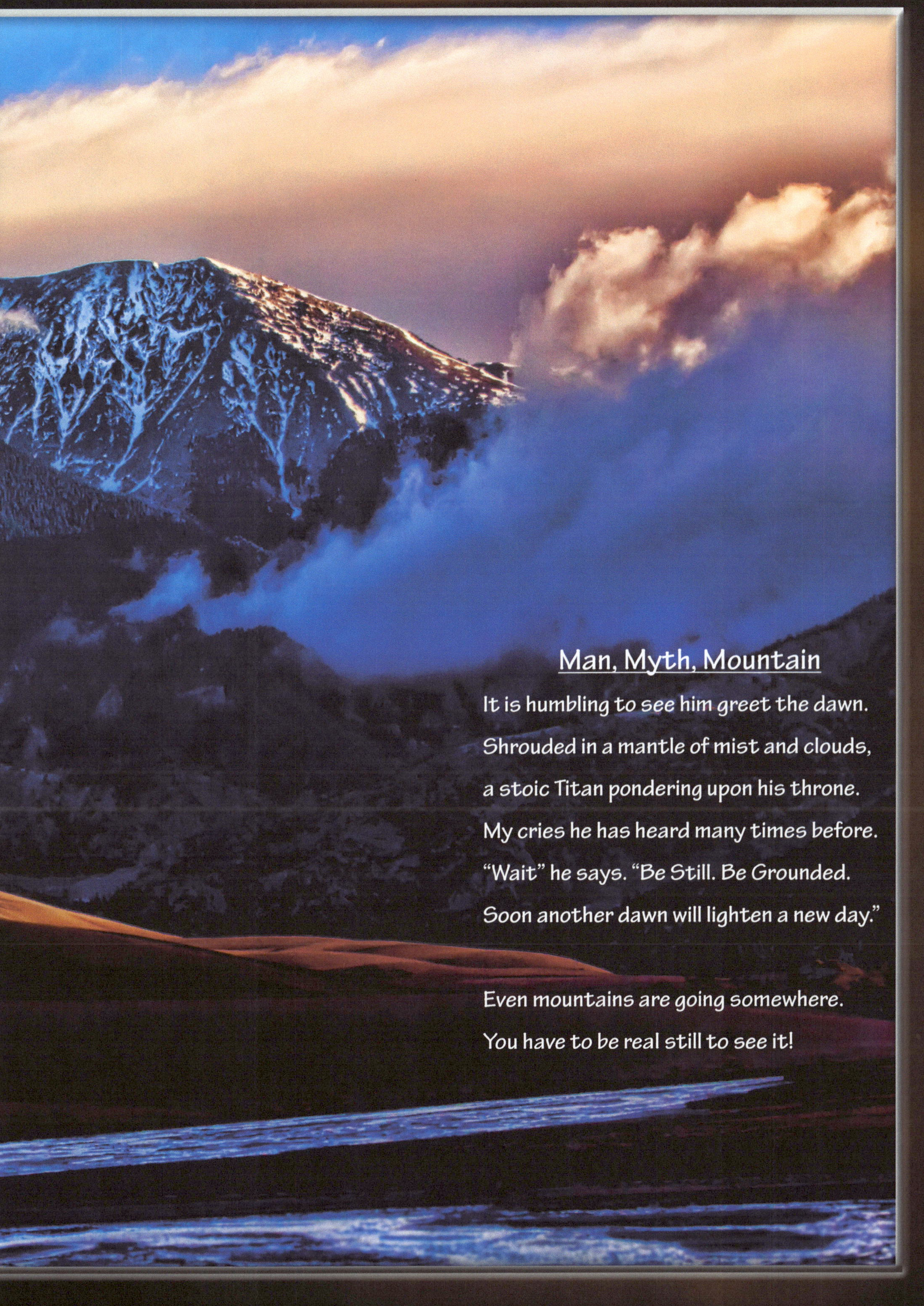

Man, Myth, Mountain

It is humbling to see him greet the dawn.
Shrouded in a mantle of mist and clouds,
a stoic Titan pondering upon his throne.
My cries he has heard many times before.
"Wait" he says. "Be Still. Be Grounded.
Soon another dawn will lighten a new day."

Even mountains are going somewhere.
You have to be real still to see it!

Temporal

I stand at the summit and shout,
"I was here!"
The wind and sand don't listen.

The only lasting footprints we leave
are in the hearts and minds of
those we've touched.
A selfless deed echoes in eternity.

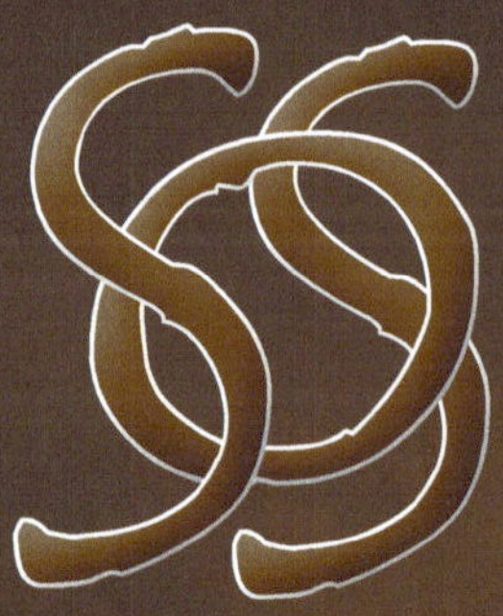

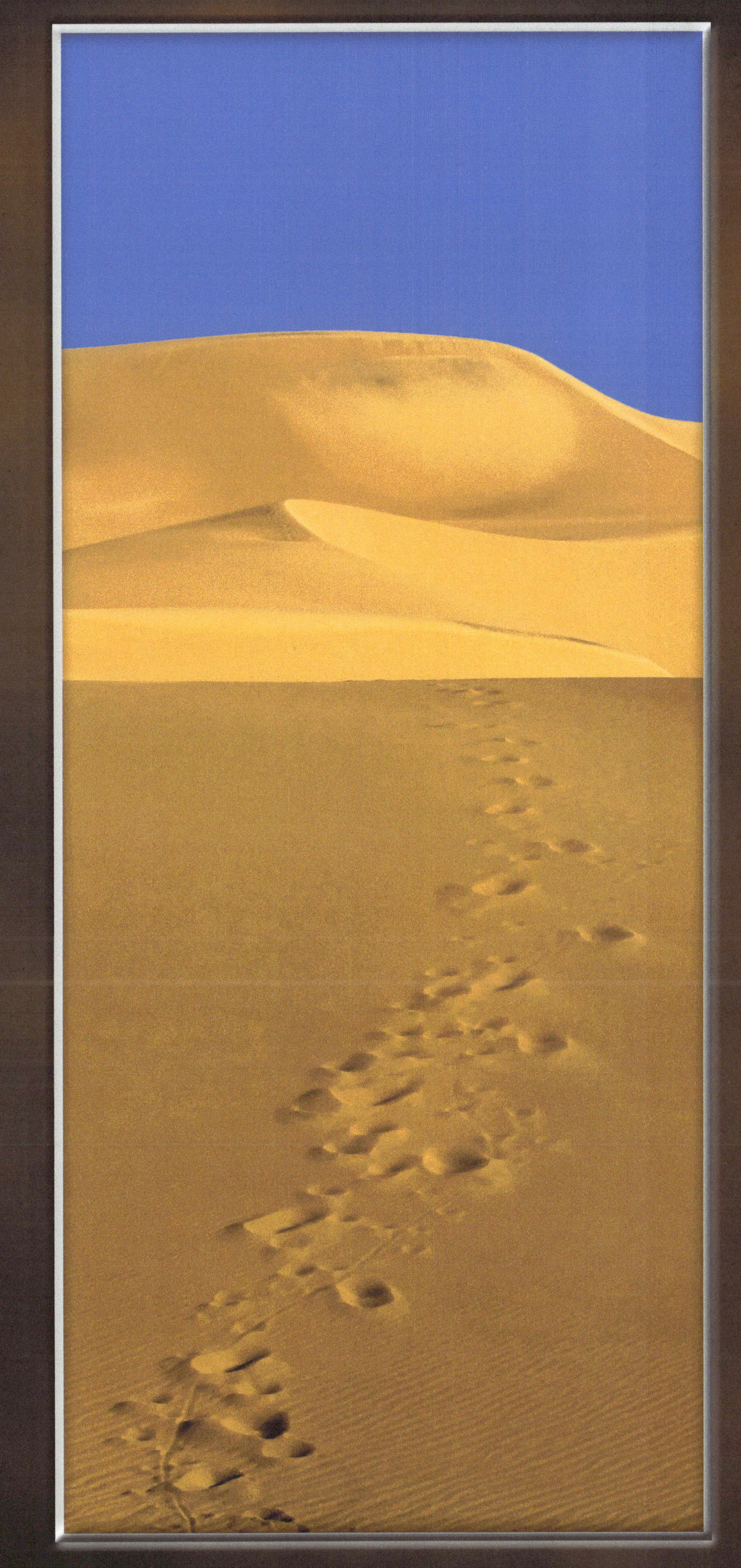

Tunnel Vision

Step after step, fixated on a goal.
We miss that which is all around us.
Playful sculptures of sand and wind.
Intricate tapestries of light and shadow.
Eyes wide shut, we keep trudging along.

Shifting Shadows

Shadows cast on shifting sand.
In a moment, both will be different.

We have just this moment. Only today.
Soon the sands will shift and move away.
The shadows we cast are different each day.

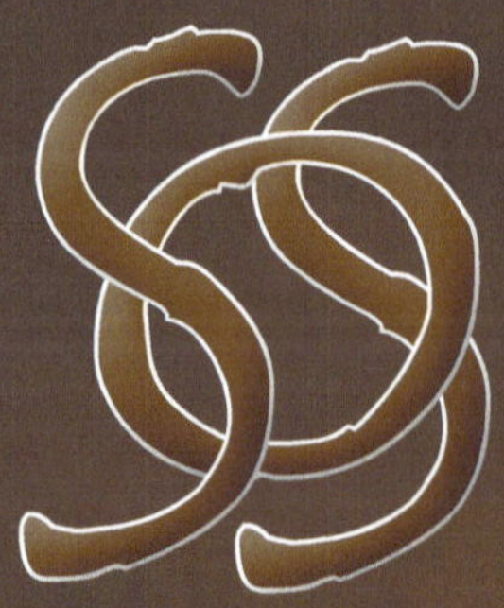

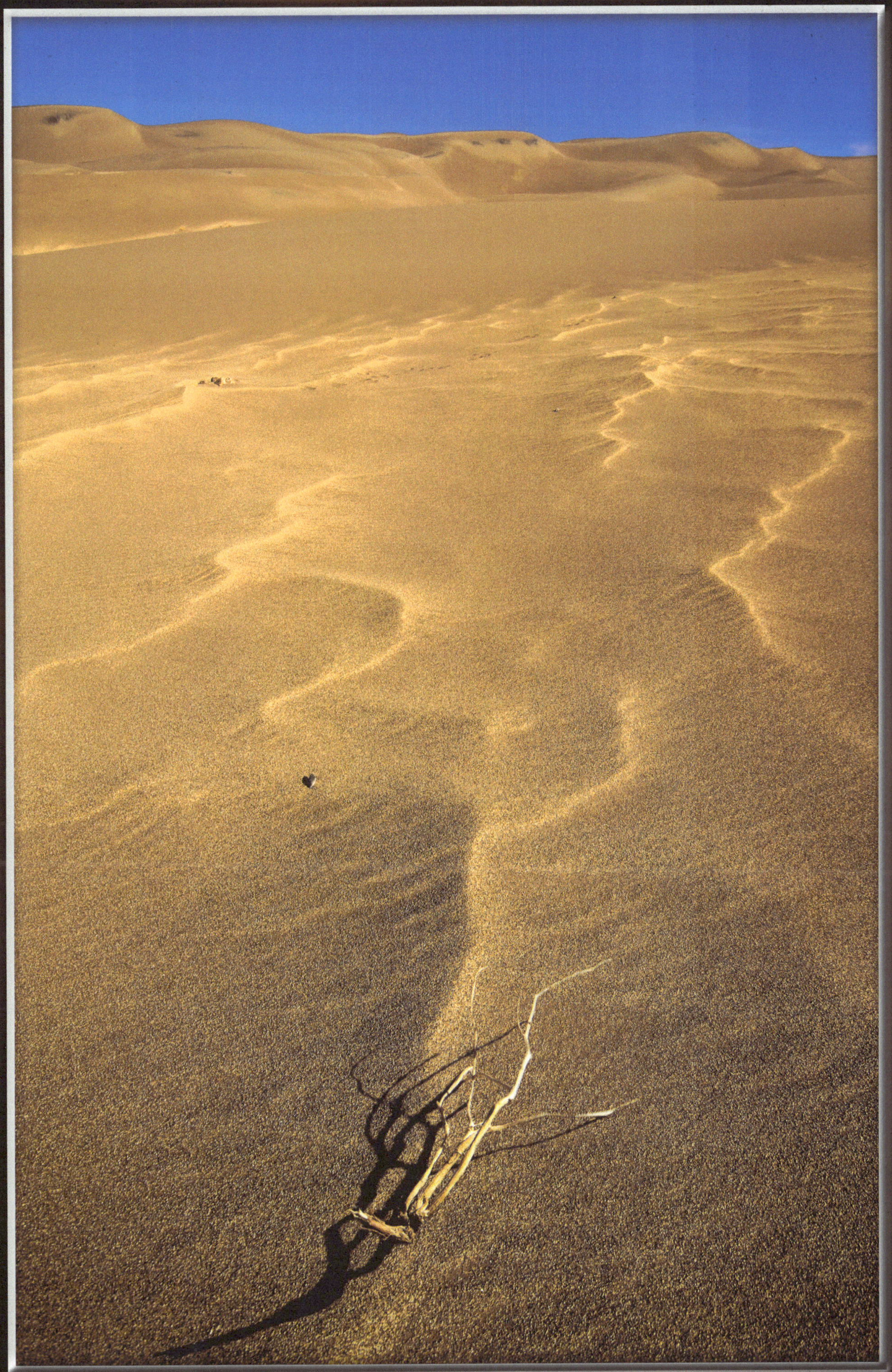

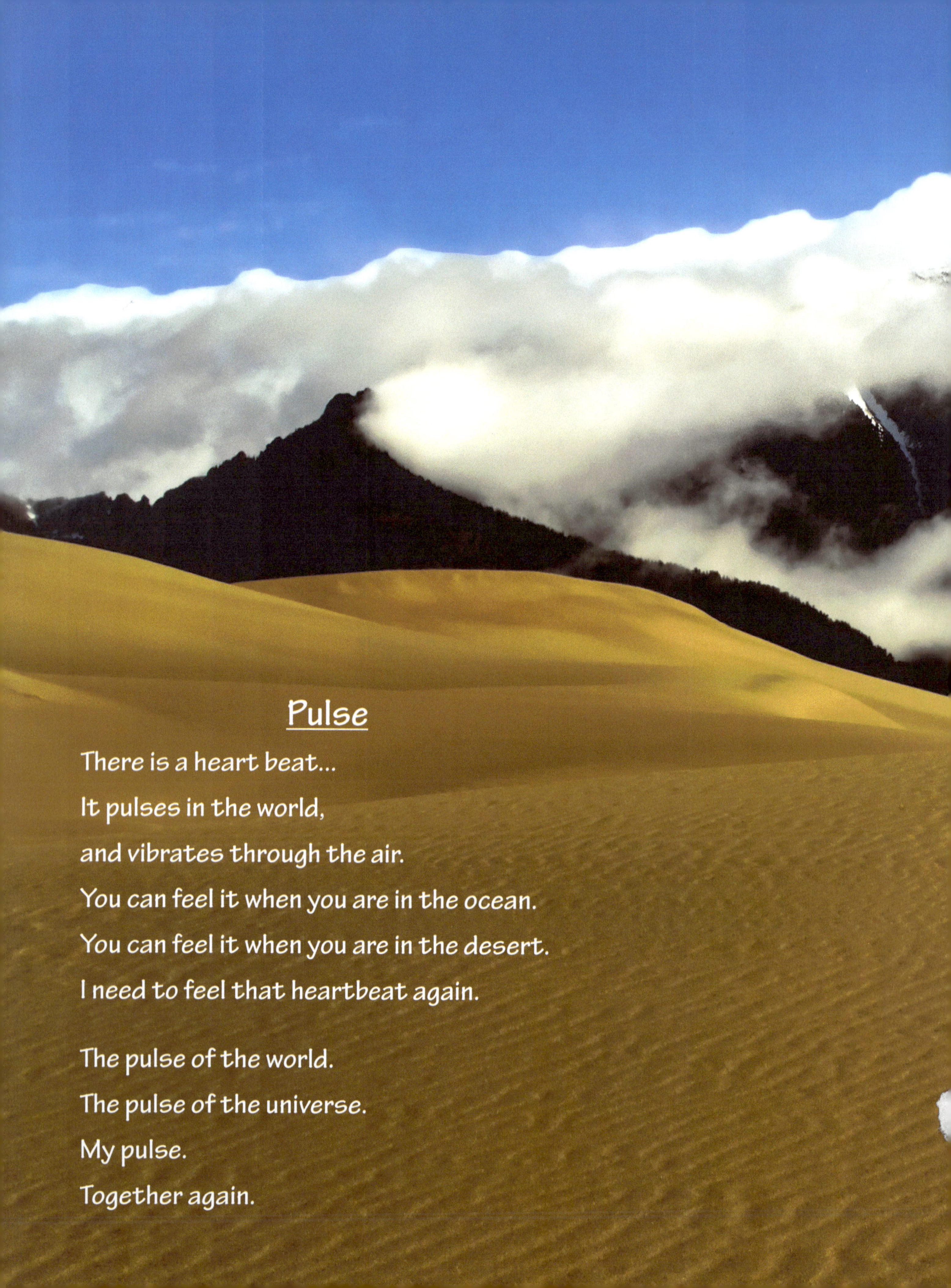

Pulse

There is a heart beat...
It pulses in the world,
and vibrates through the air.
You can feel it when you are in the ocean.
You can feel it when you are in the desert.
I need to feel that heartbeat again.

The pulse of the world.
The pulse of the universe.
My pulse.
Together again.

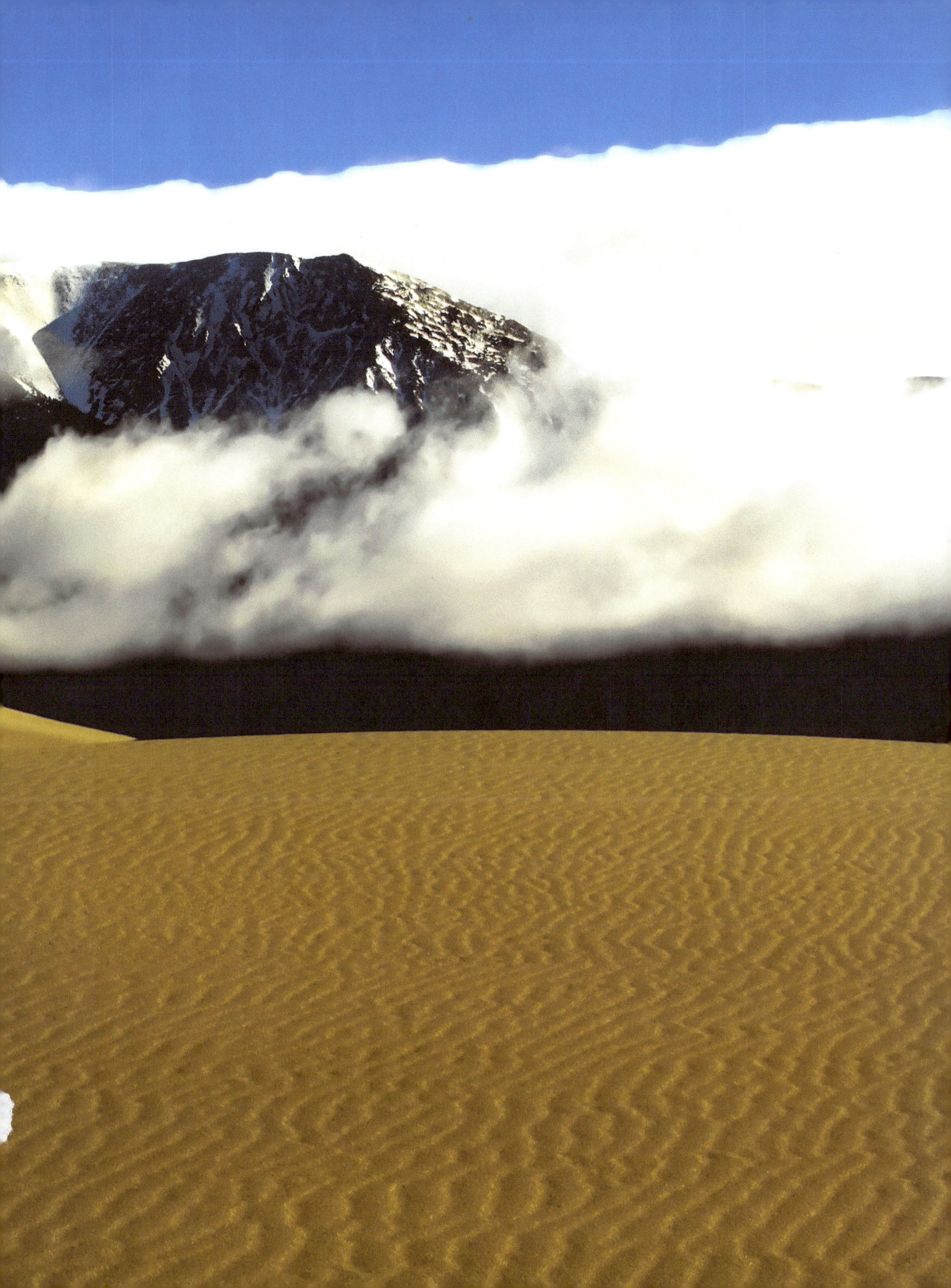

Sound of Silence

Monument Valley Navajo Tribal Park

Northern New Mexico / Southern Arizona

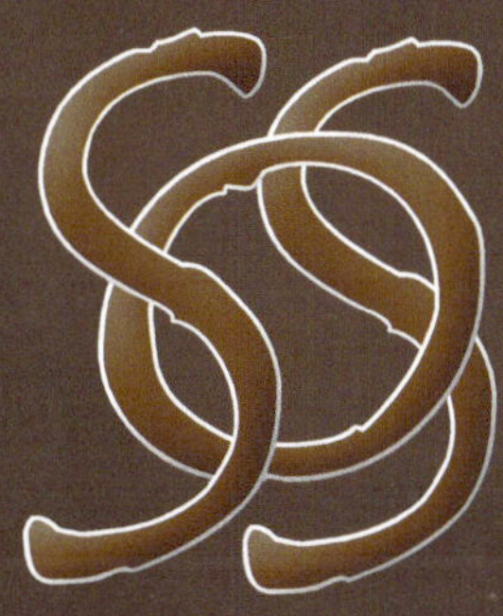

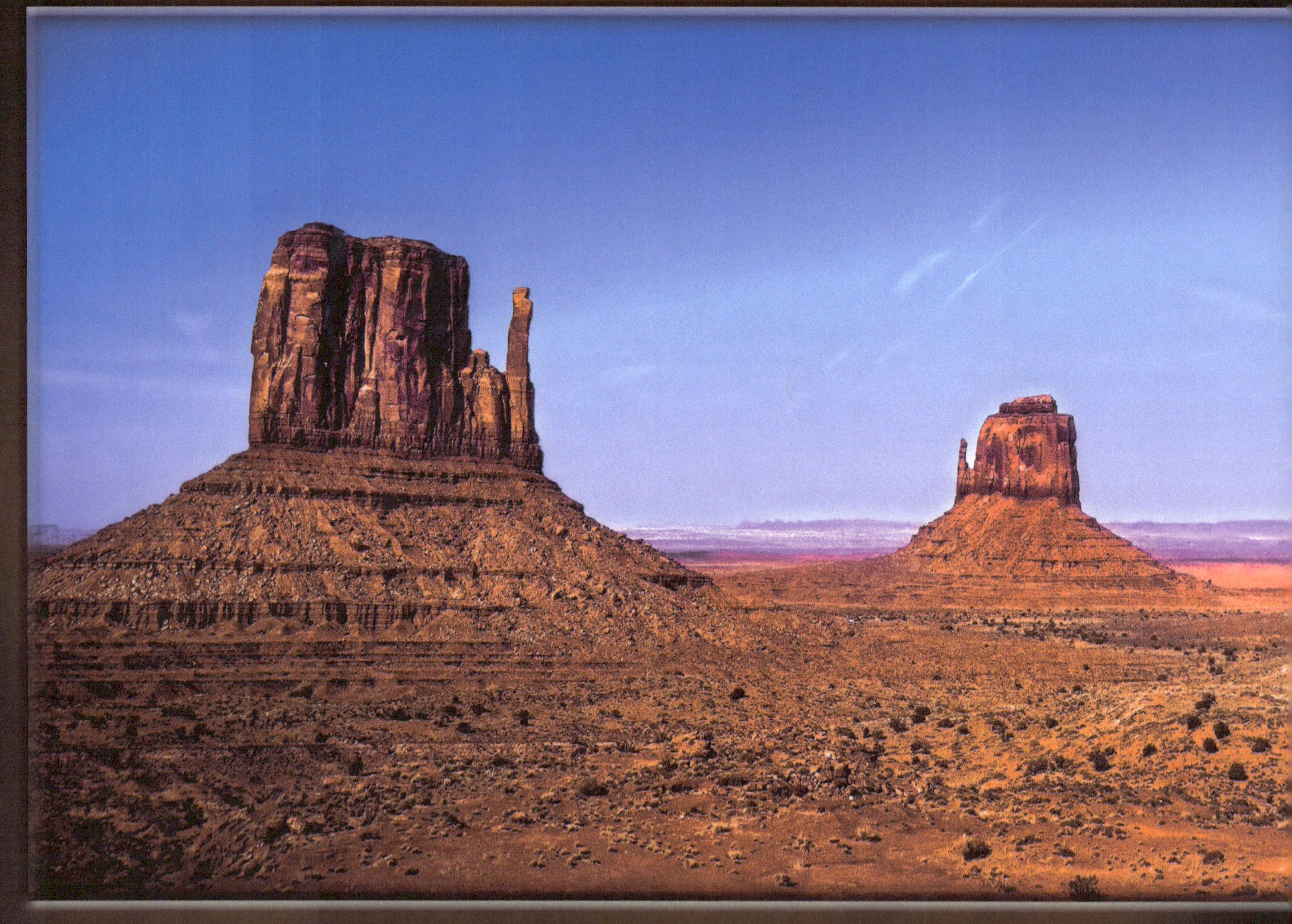

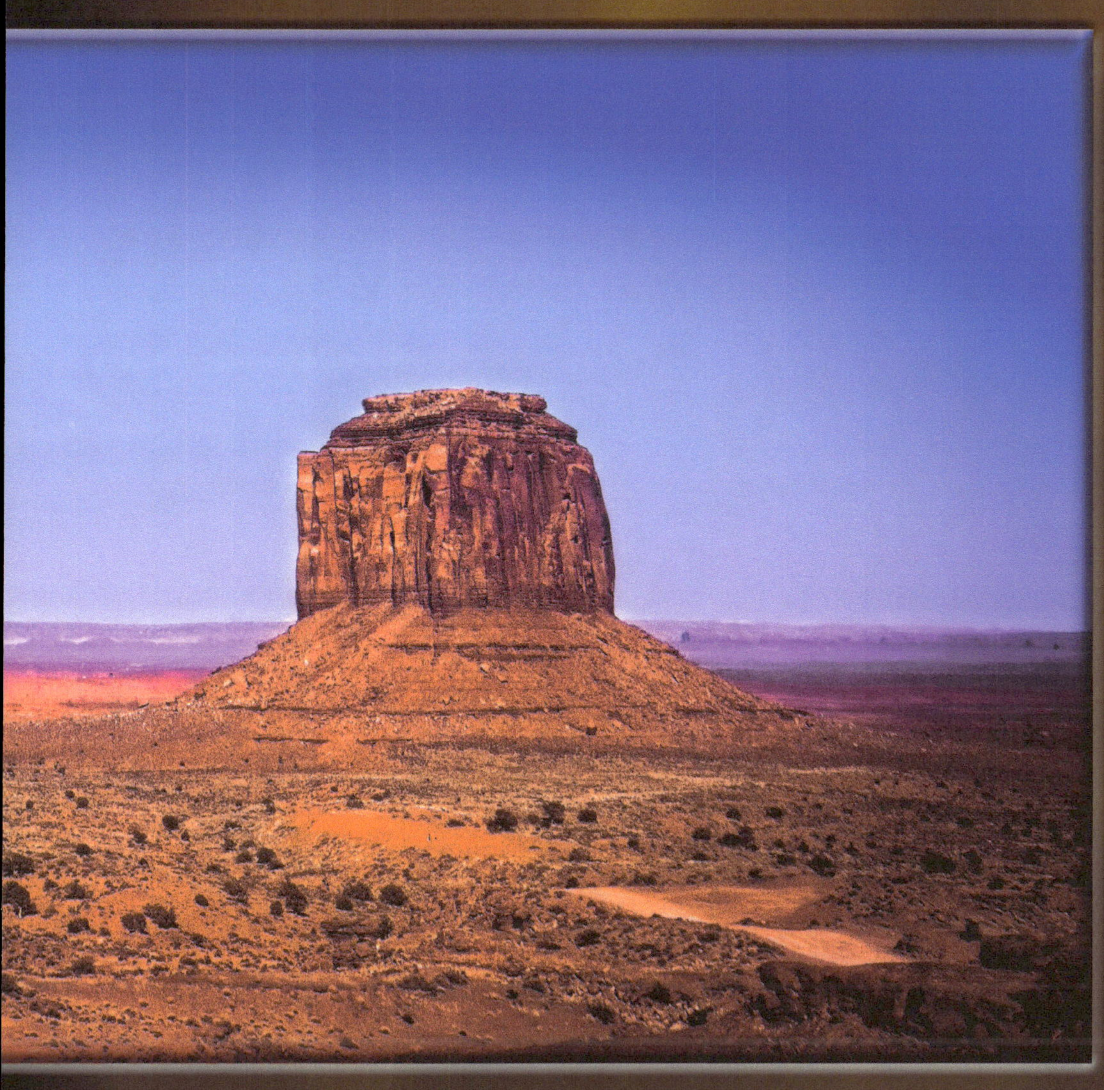

These Three Remain

. . . And the greatest of these is love.

Surrounded by breathtaking beauty,

we think of those we love.

It's why we are here.

To love more than we hate.

To give more than we take.

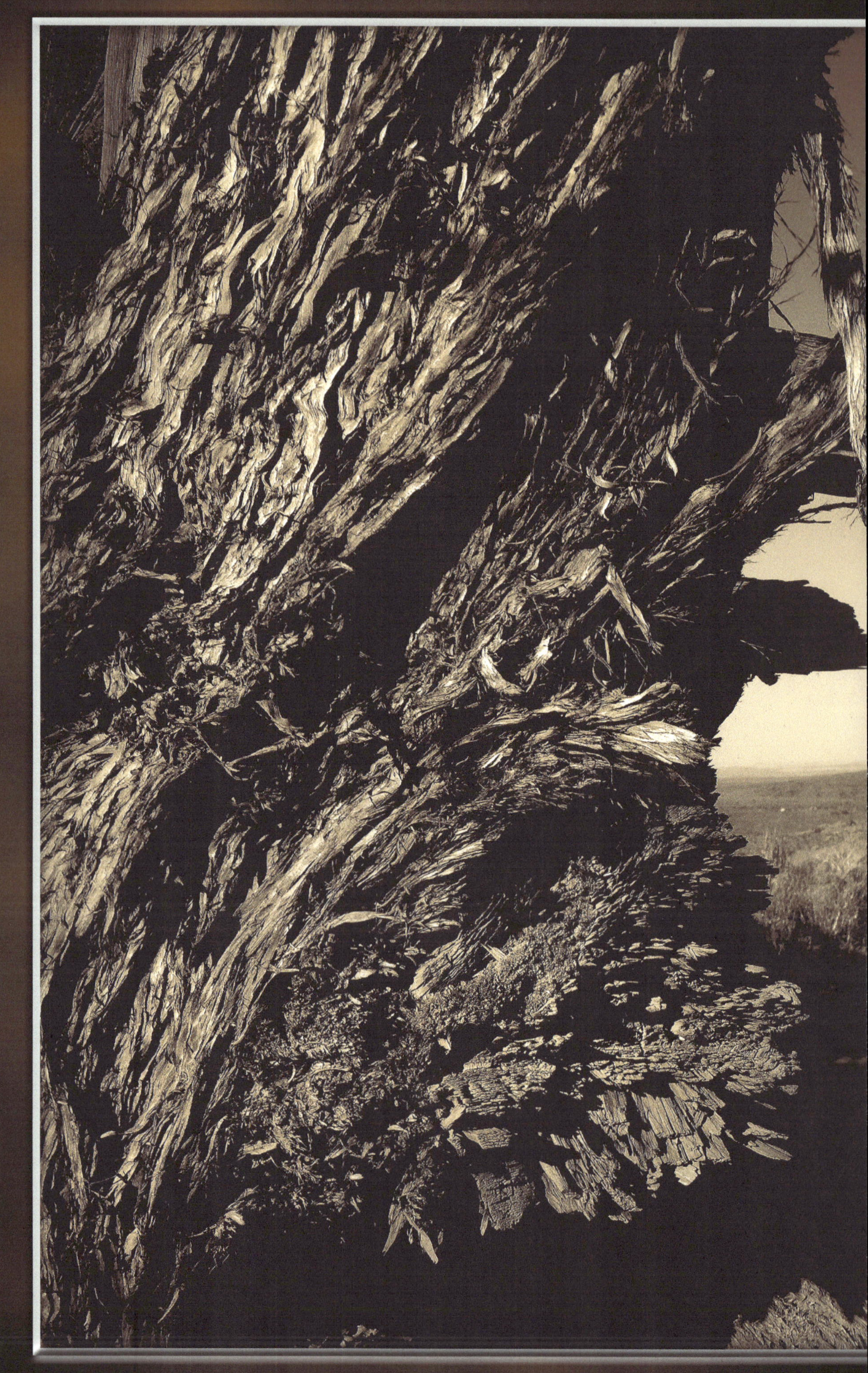

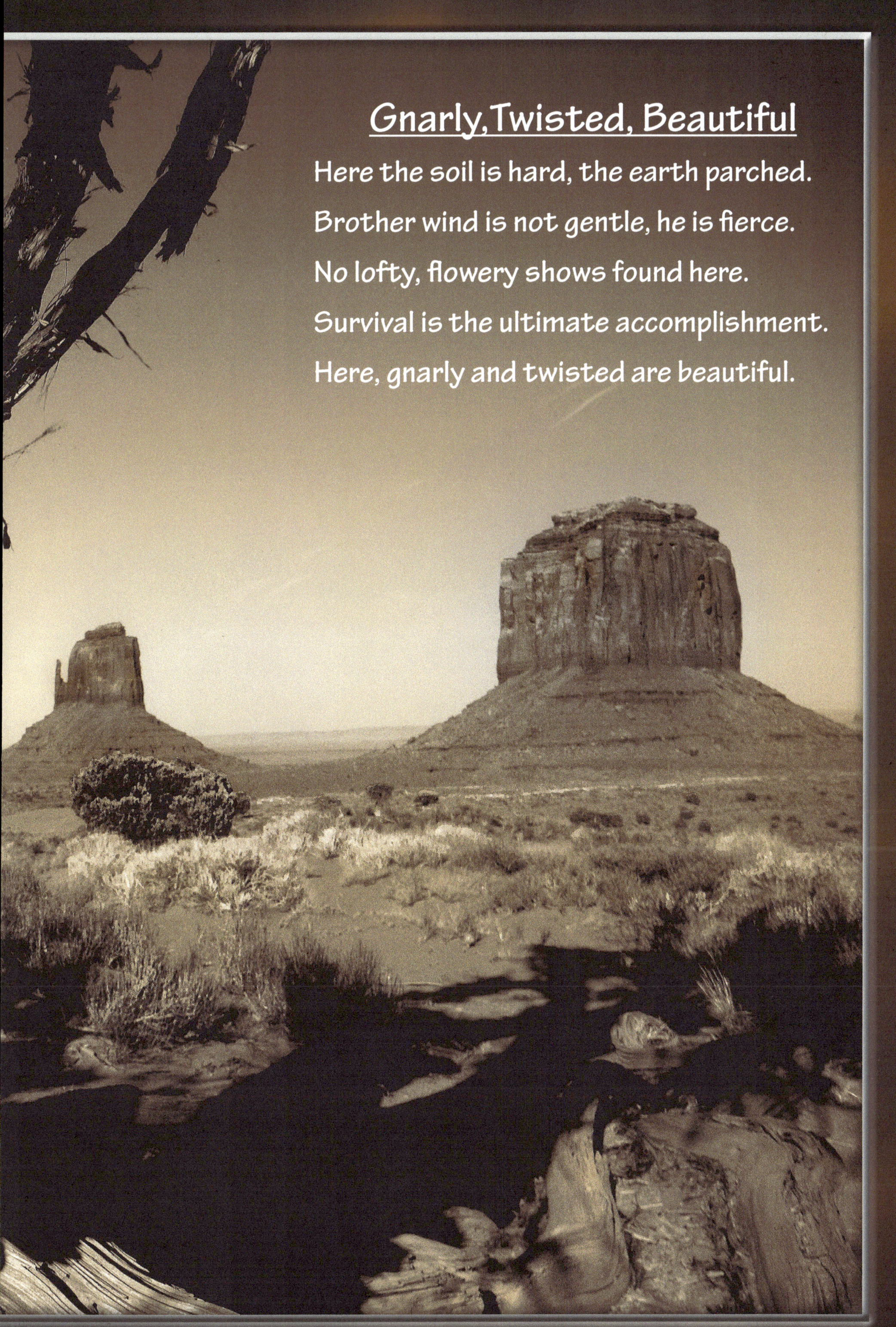

Gnarly,Twisted, Beautiful

Here the soil is hard, the earth parched.
Brother wind is not gentle, he is fierce.
No lofty, flowery shows found here.
Survival is the ultimate accomplishment.
Here, gnarly and twisted are beautiful.

Awakening

Learning to see again. To open your eyes.
To see the presence of beauty around you
is a first step toward freedom from despair.

Even eyes of stone appreciate flowers.

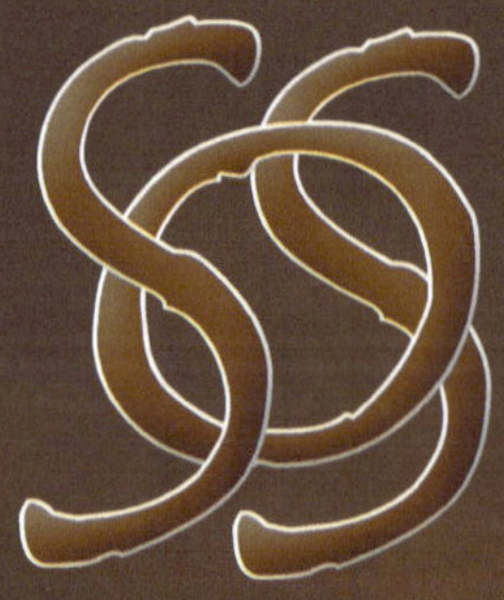

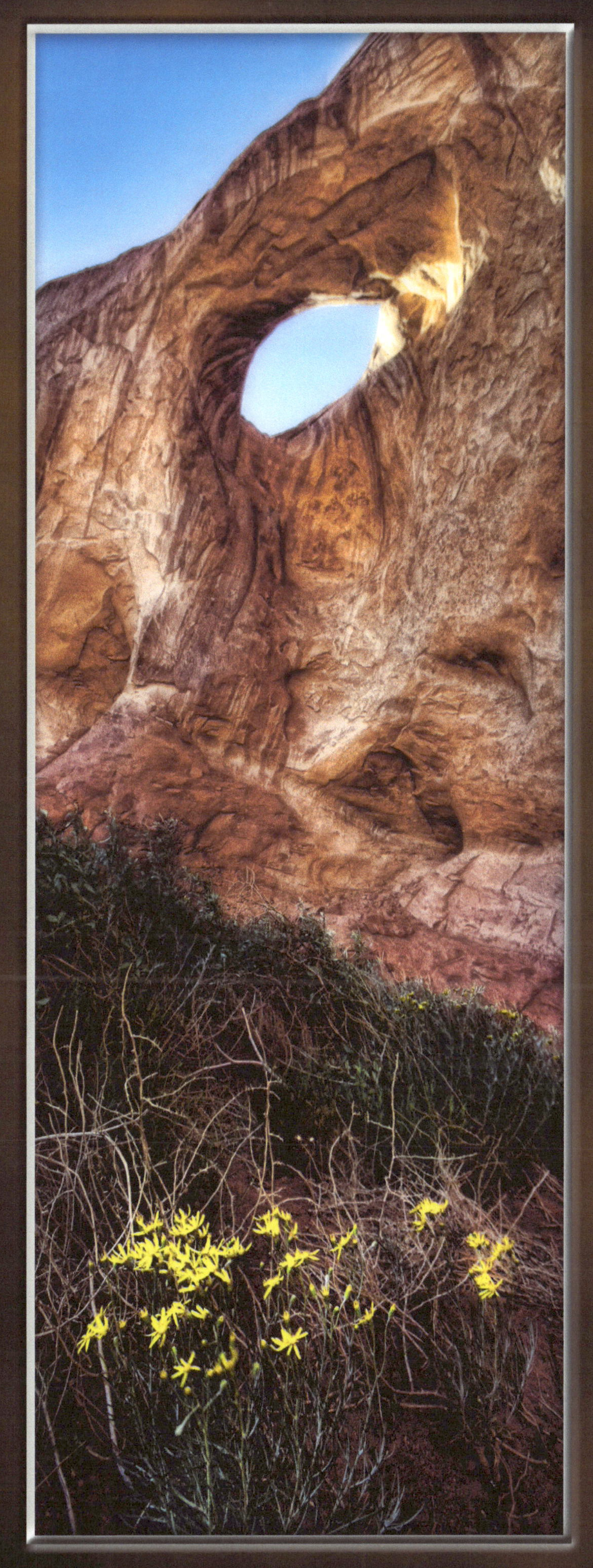

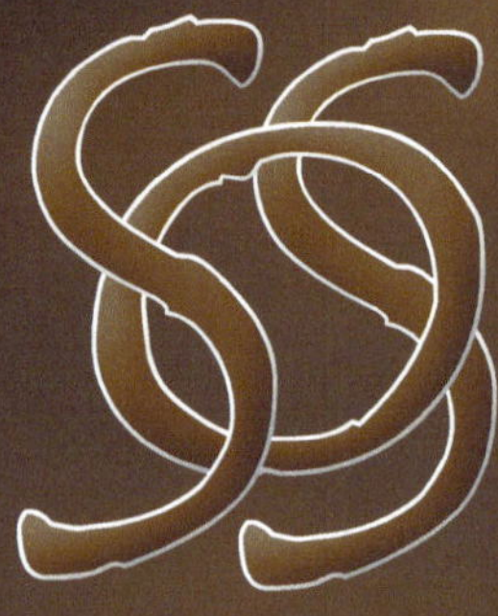

GodEye

How shall we see today?
Our eyes?
Here today,
gone tomorrow.
God's eye?
Eye of stone:
patient, enduring,
centuries, millennia,
stoically observing.

"To the caterpillar, it is the end of the world.
To the sage it's the birth of a butterfly." - Tao Te Ching

Nothing is a crisis to the eternal...

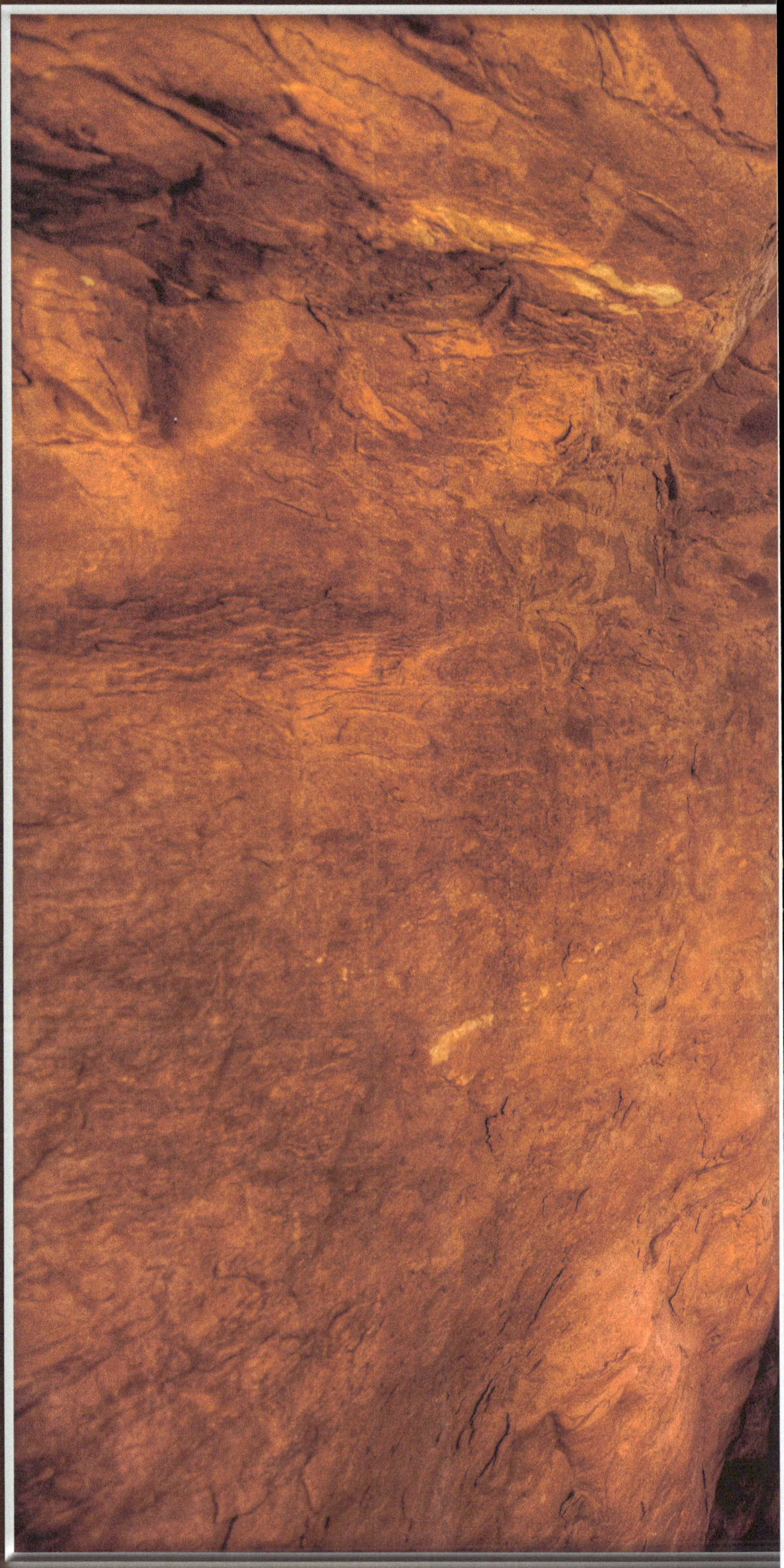

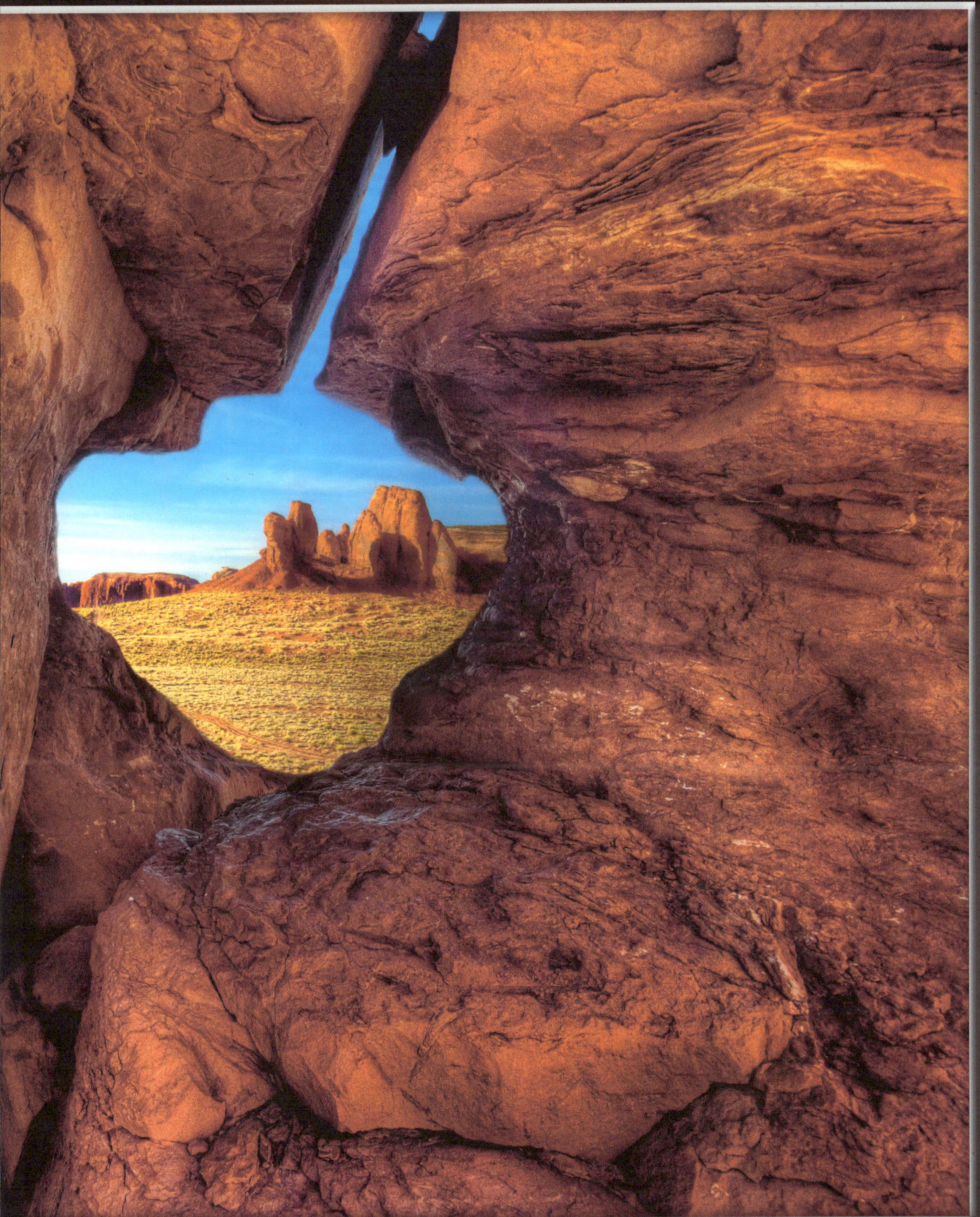

So Be It

Mr. B. doesn't know he can't climb it.

Nor will he feel sorry for himself when he can't.

He will simply let go and move on.

Beetles are philosophical masters of,

"It is what it is."

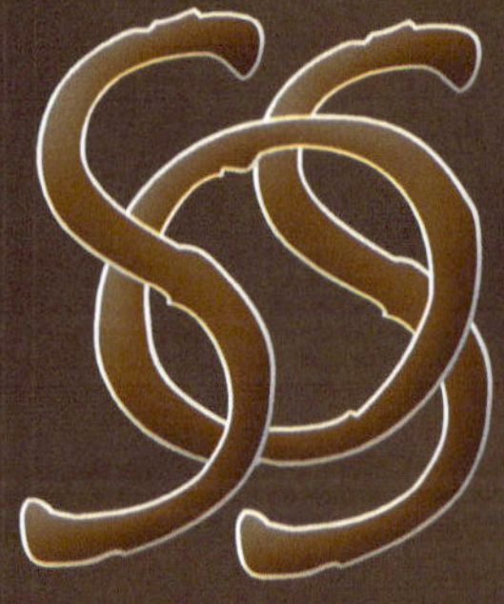

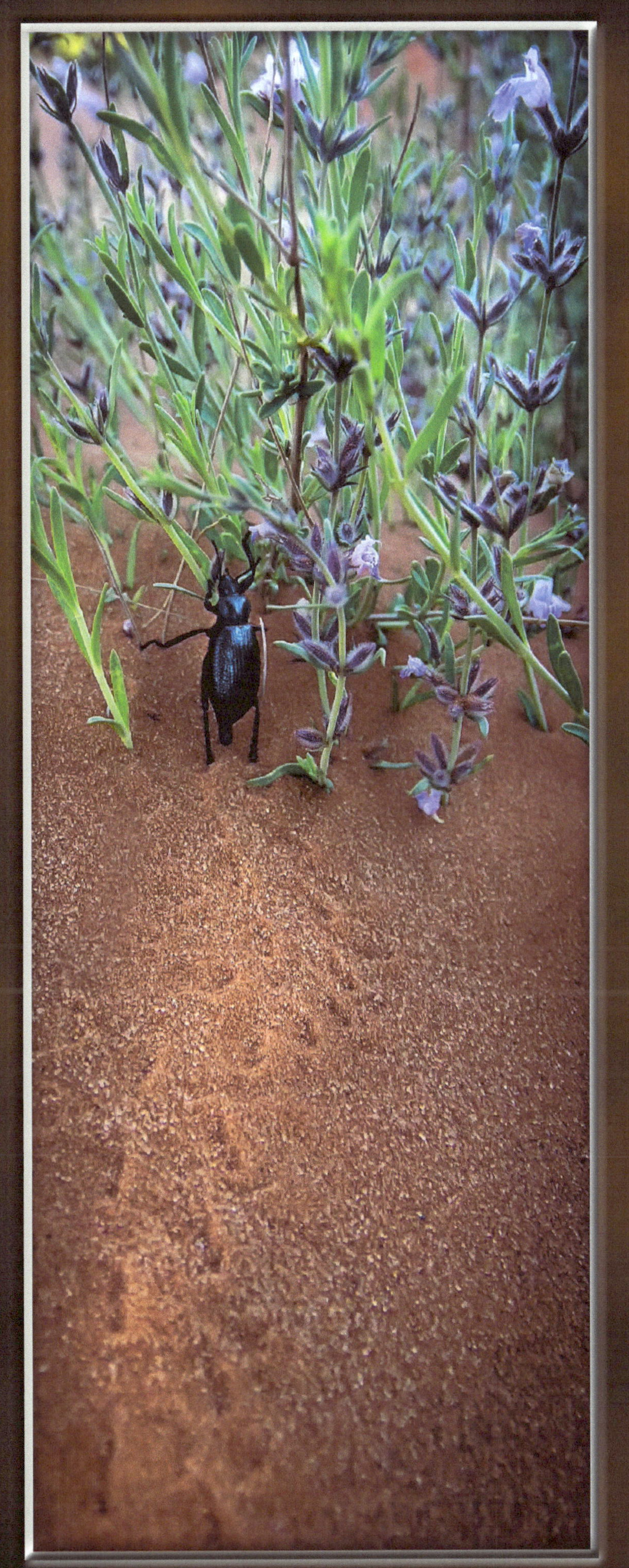

KISS, KISS, KISS

The buzz of the world
can be too much...
Simplify. Simplify. Simplify.
Strip out the loud colors.
See the form beneath.
No less beautiful-
Just different.

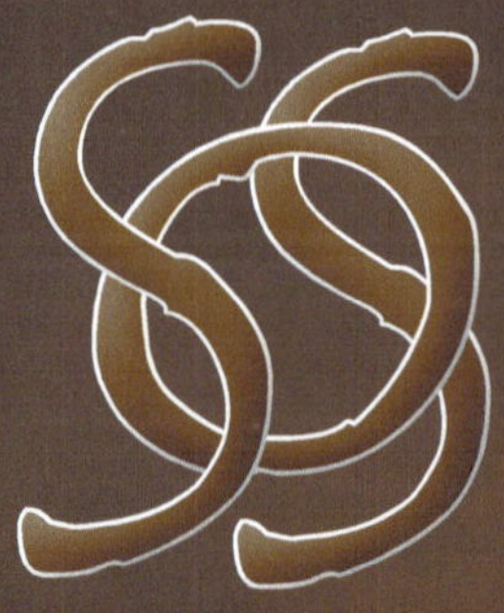

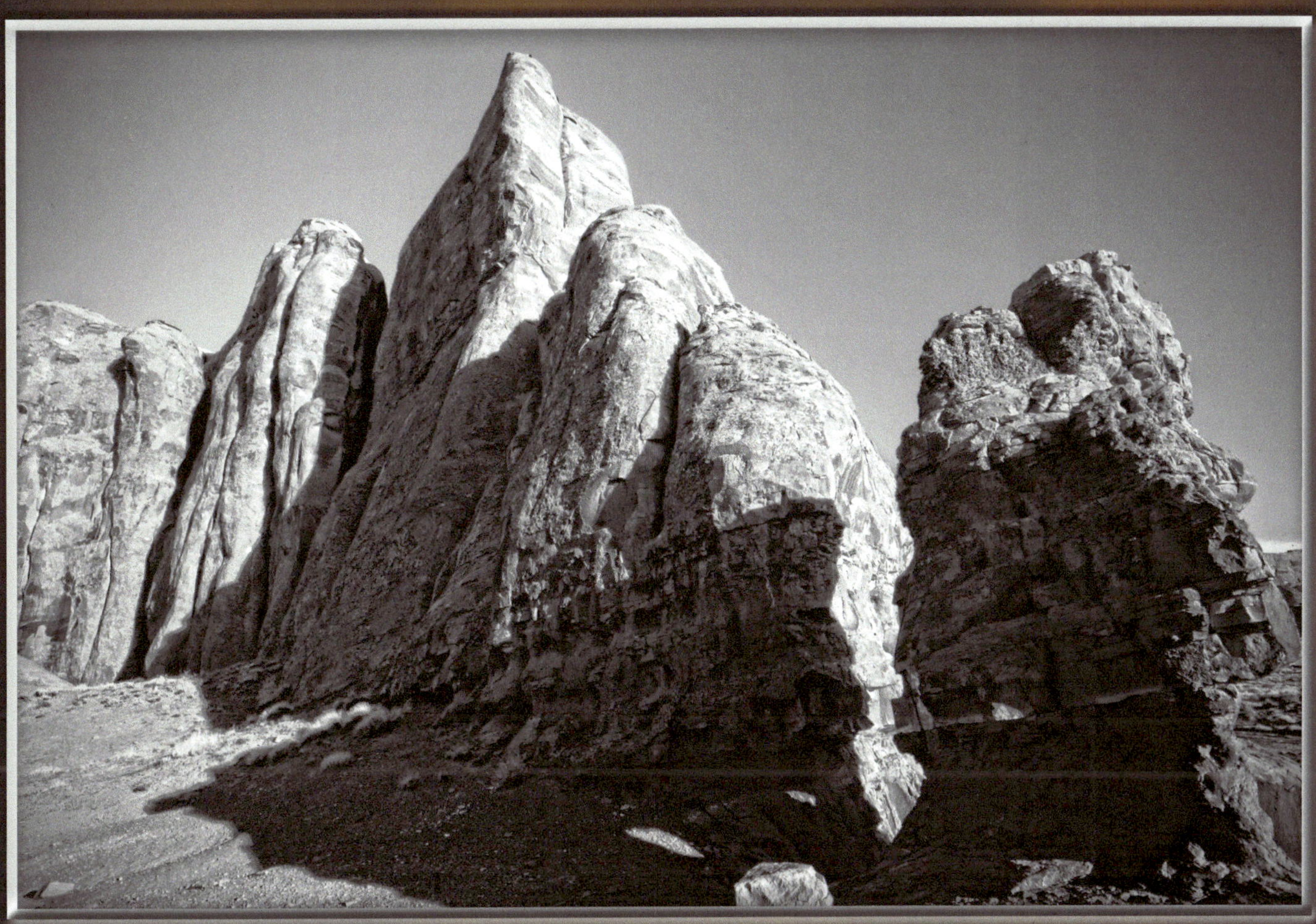

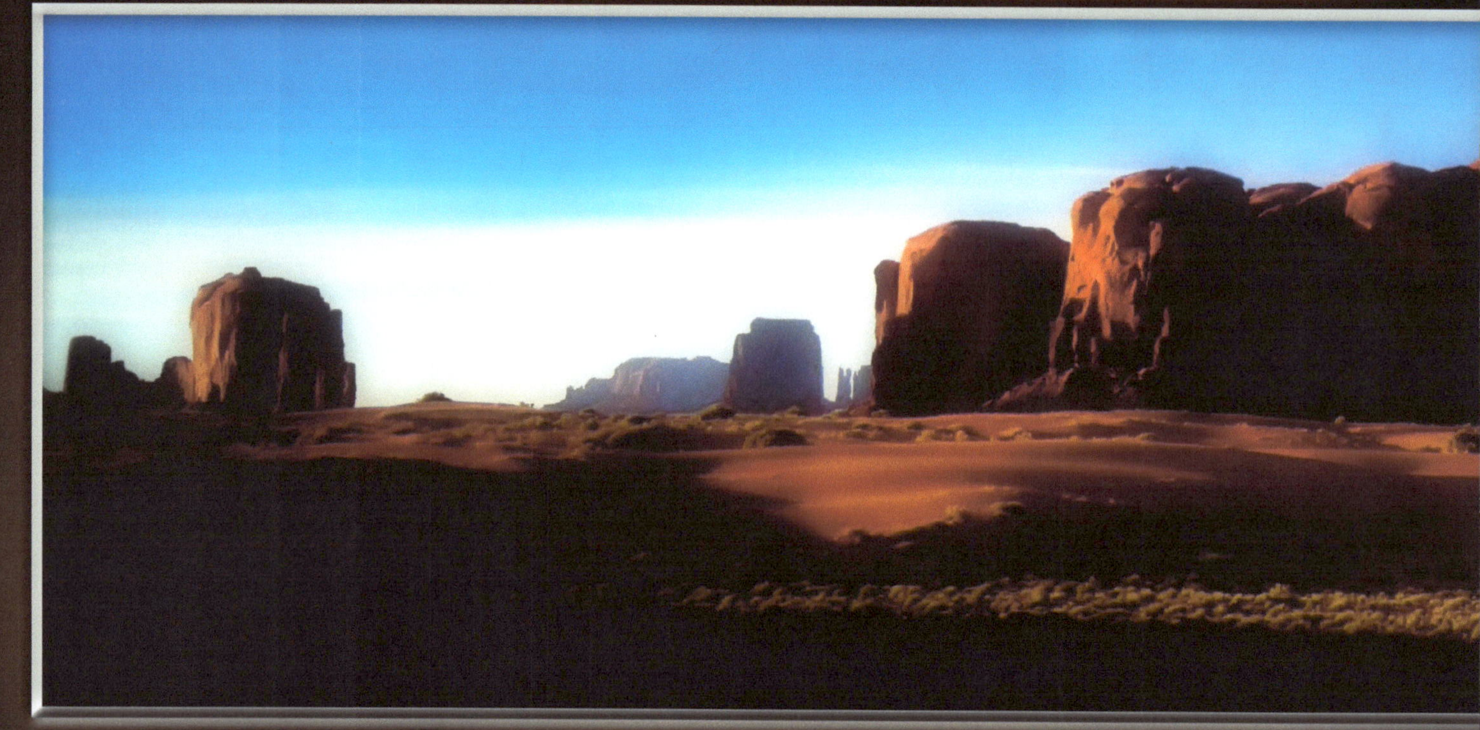

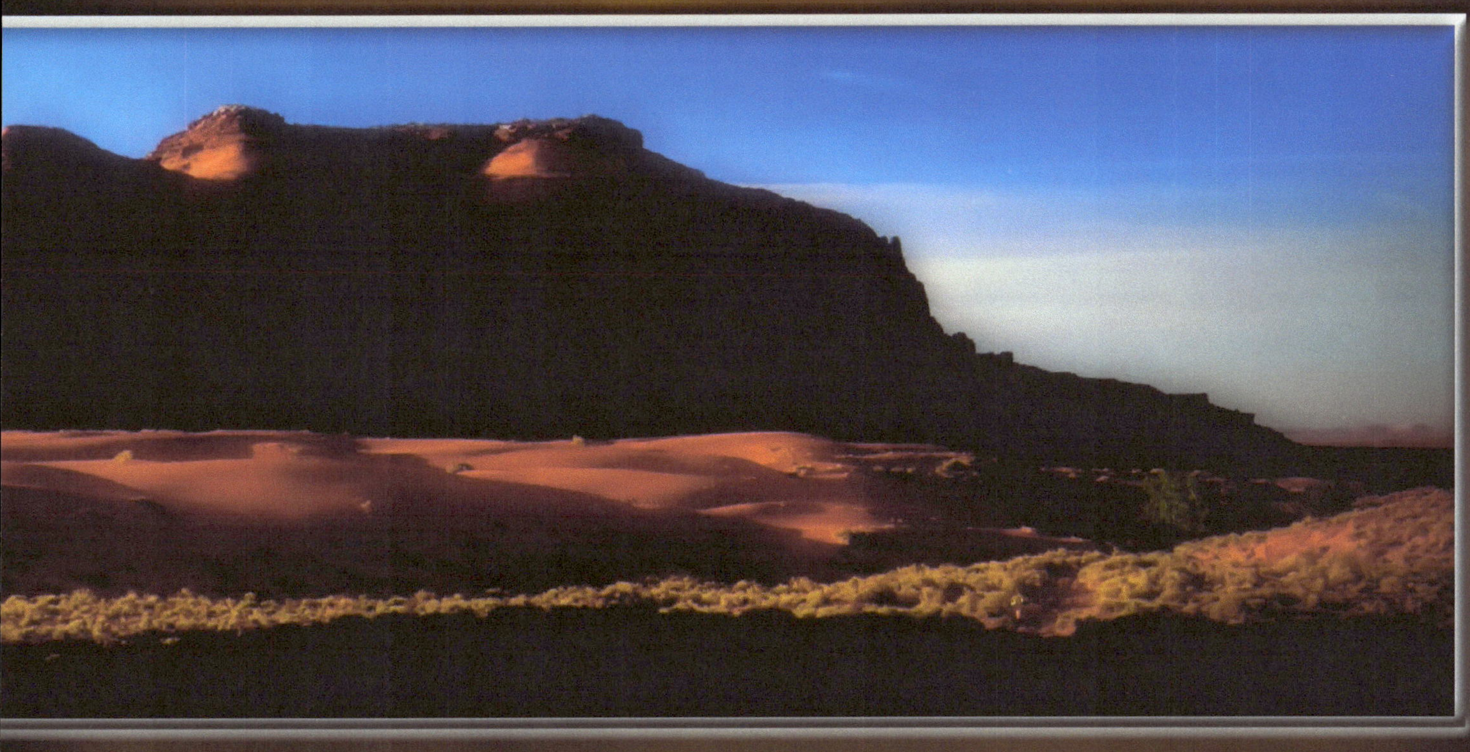

Distant Shadows

Shadows reveal the depths of things.
They make light more beautiful.
Spend too long in darkness and
you can begin to fear the light.
Some shadows are better
appreciated from a distance.

Wisdom

Wizened by time and patinated by desert,
The limbs of an ancient one speak to me:
"You will come join me here someday.
Did you live your life well?
Did you persevere drought and storm?
Did you rejoice at the touch of rain?
Did your laughter float upon the breeze?"

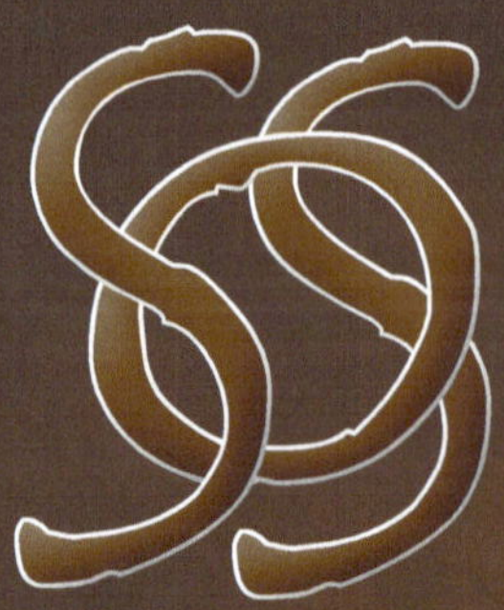

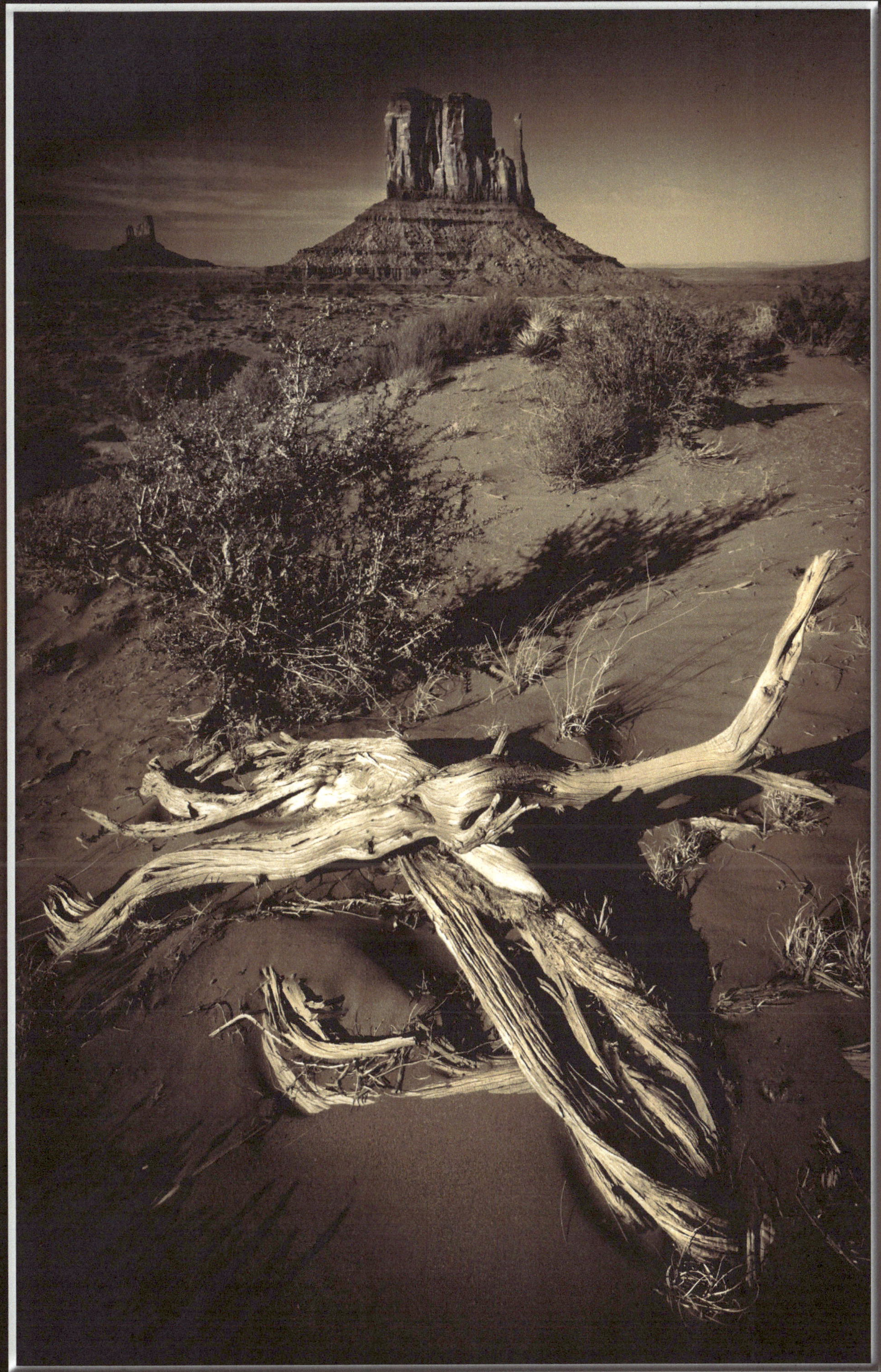

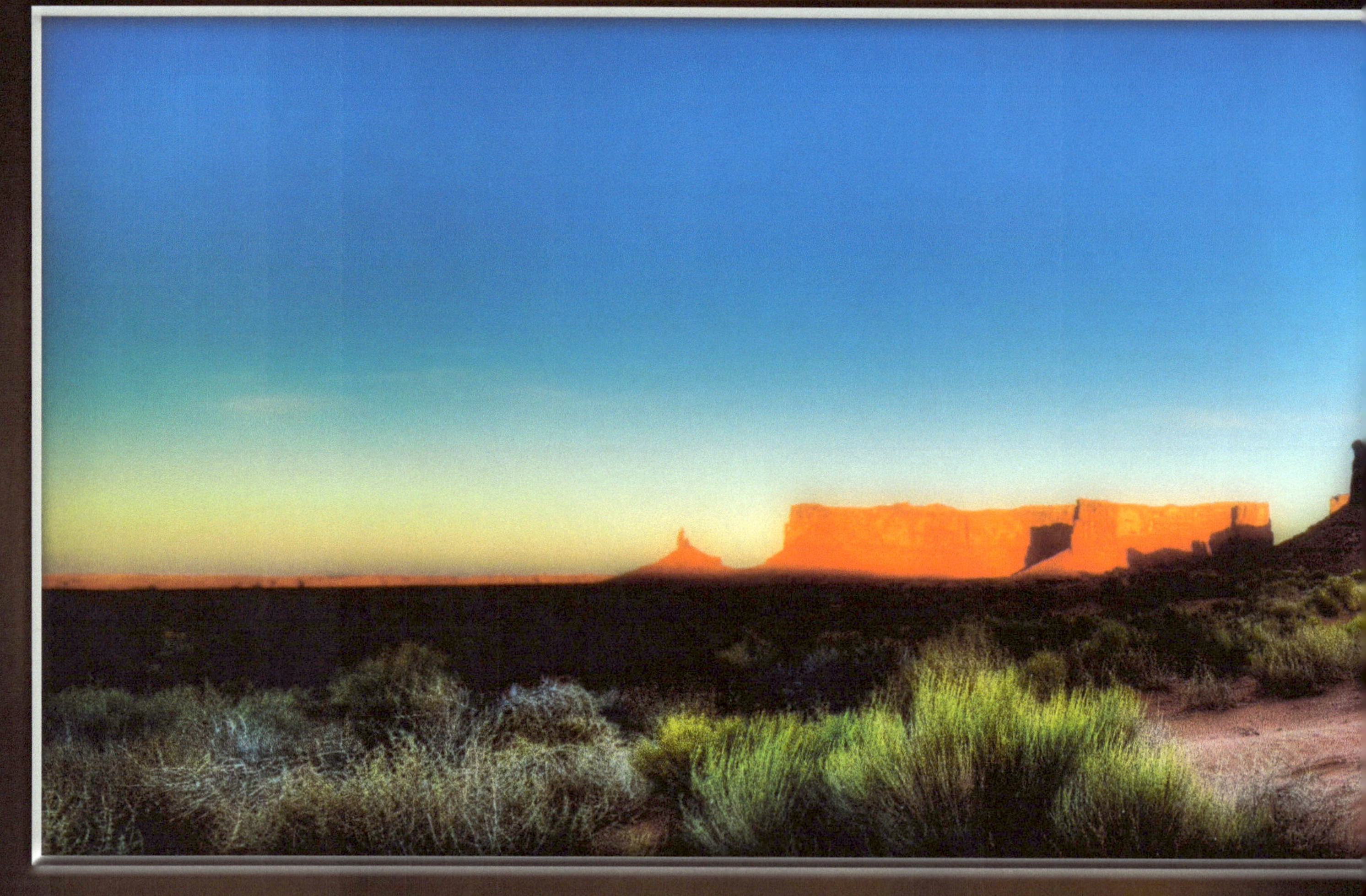

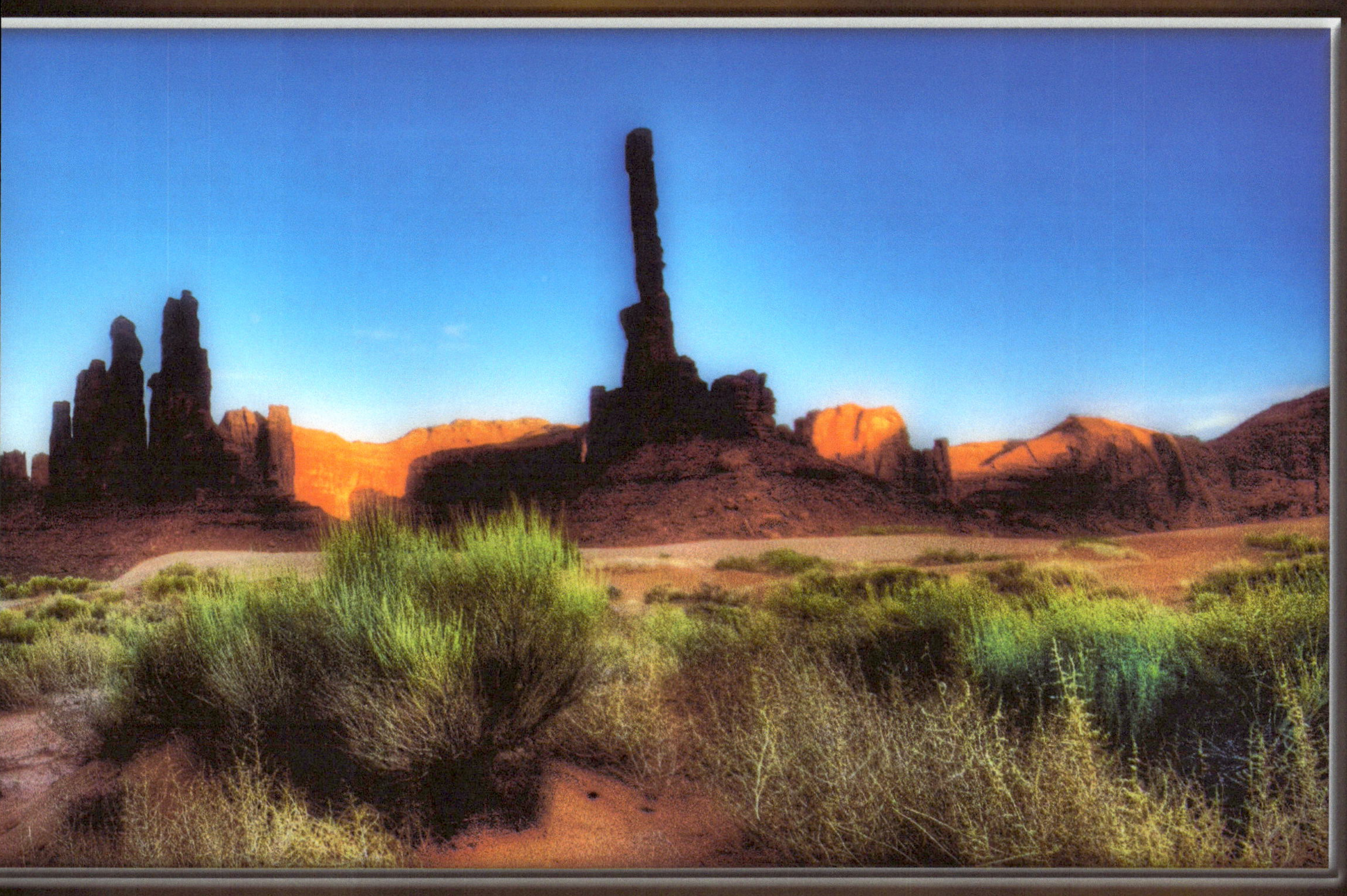

powered by SOL

If the sun were to represent the Universal Spirit,

then the moon would represent the individual soul.

Not only because it is a reflection of the sun's light,

but because it wanes from darkness to light and back again.

Like the trials of life.

So it is the moon that governs love, poetry, music, and magick.

All capable of darkness and light.

Sound of Silence

Horseshoe Bend, Lake Powell

Northwestern Arizona

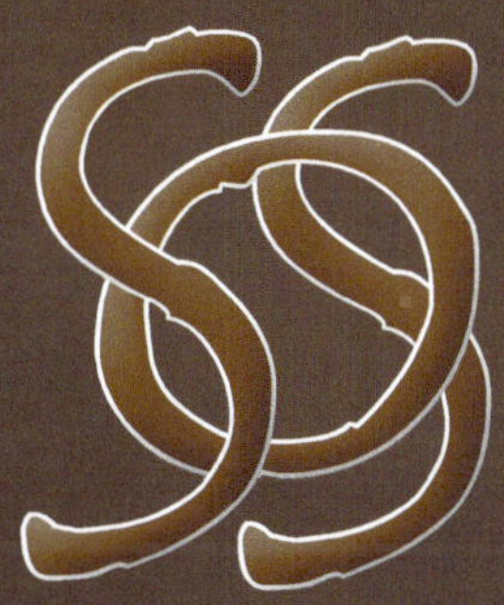

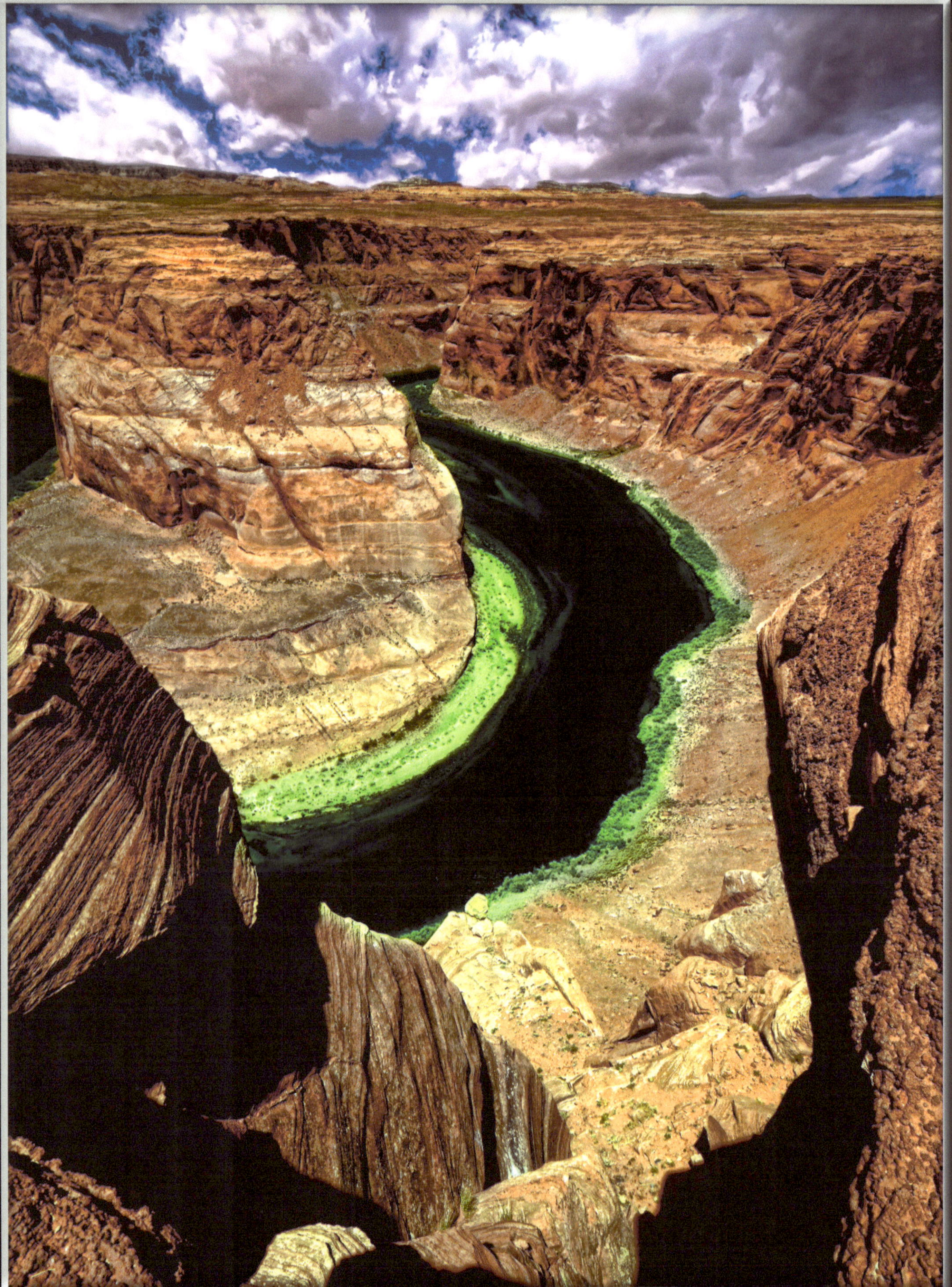

Woman Power

Water is woman power.

Bringing life to desolation.

Molding barren into beautiful.

Nurturing, Creating, Celebrating.

Enraged - Unstoppable,

Cleansing.

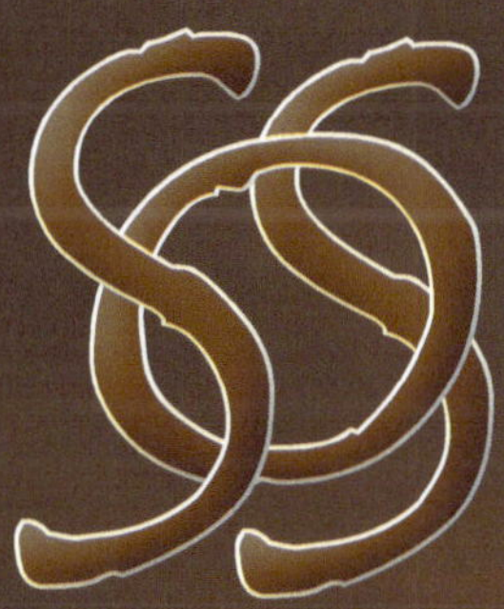

<u>Circle Of Life</u>

Inside each of us,
is a unique twinkle of
starlight,
a glimmer of a dew drop,
a glimpse of the Divine.
It is always there,
tucked in our hearts.
It may be strengthened by
our kindness
or shadowed by our fears,
but it is forever with us -
because it is us.
It is who we were before we
were born,
and it is who we will be after
we die.
We are all sacred.

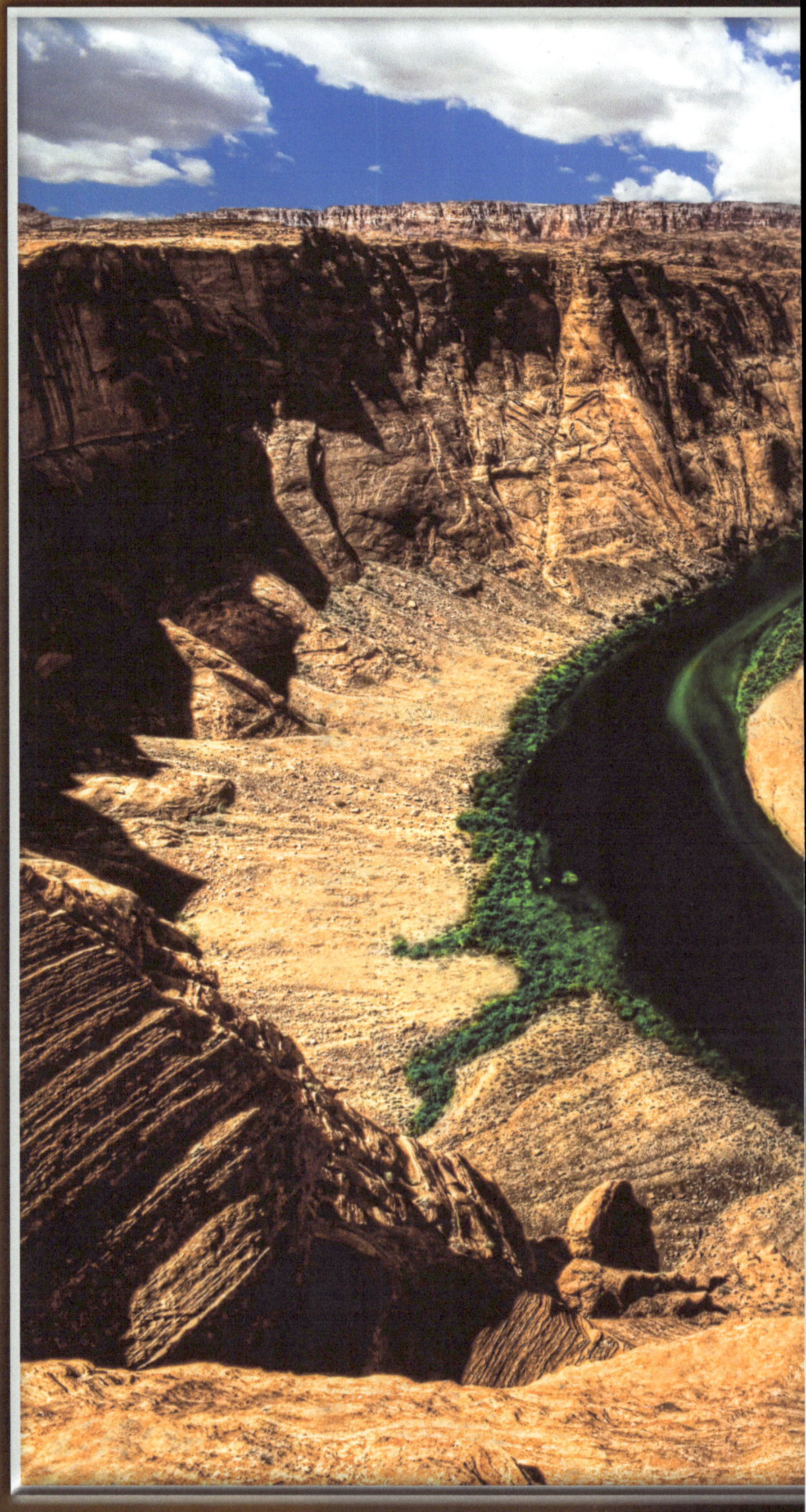

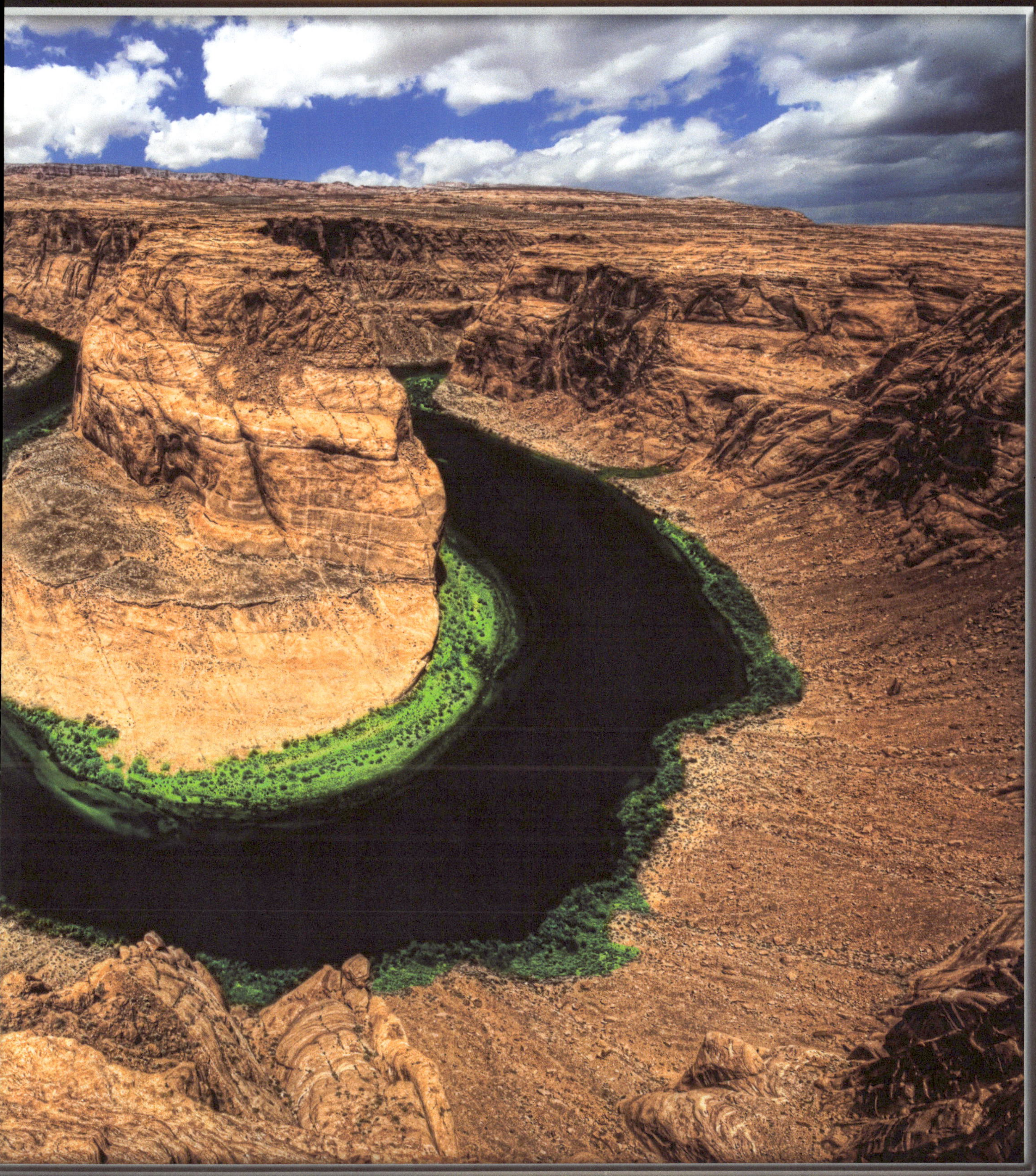

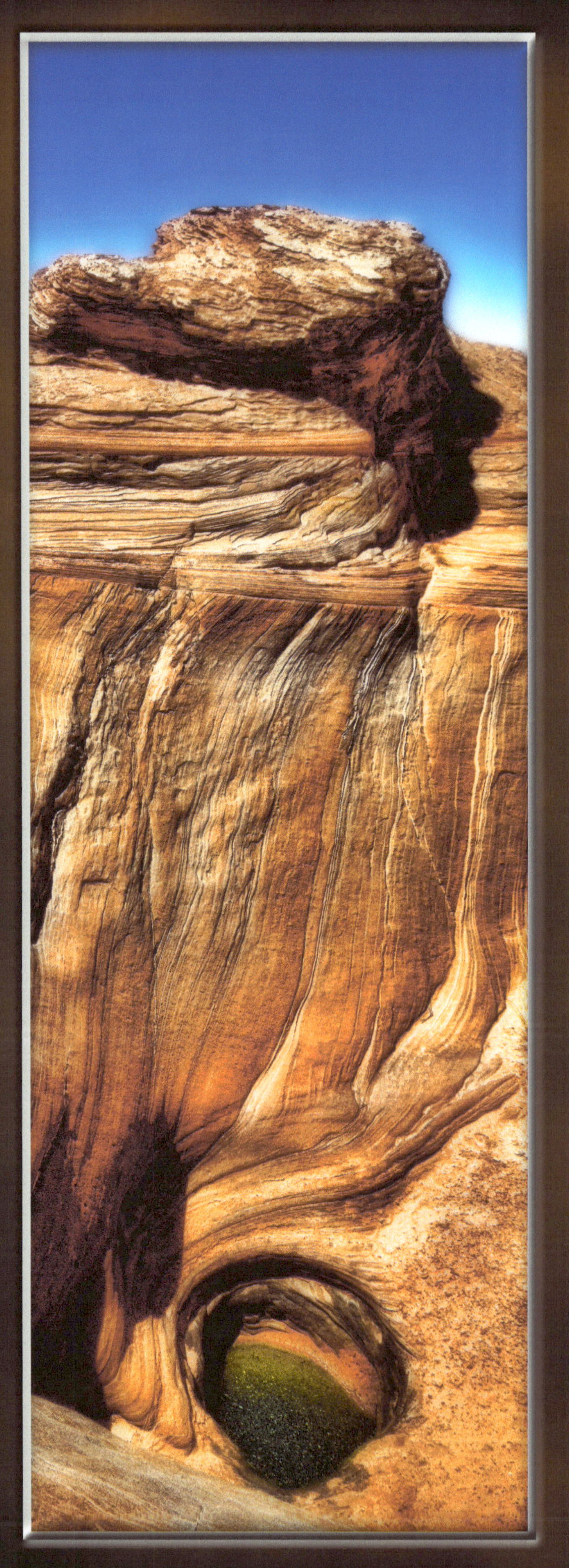

Secrets

Rock.

Shelf upon shelf of rock.

Endless. Unchanging.

Then appears a secret well.

Secrets can look so pretty,

But their water makes you sick.

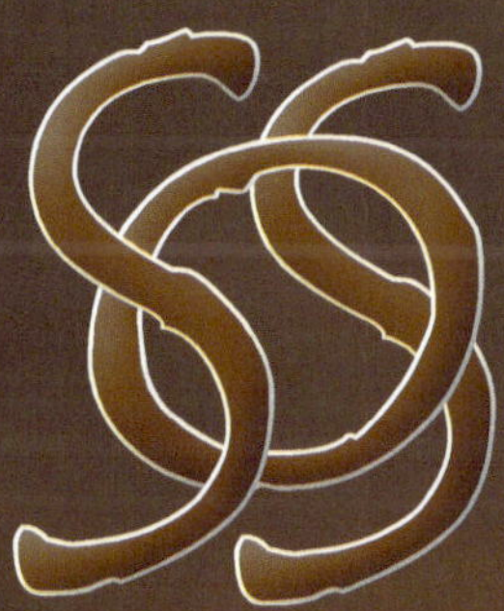

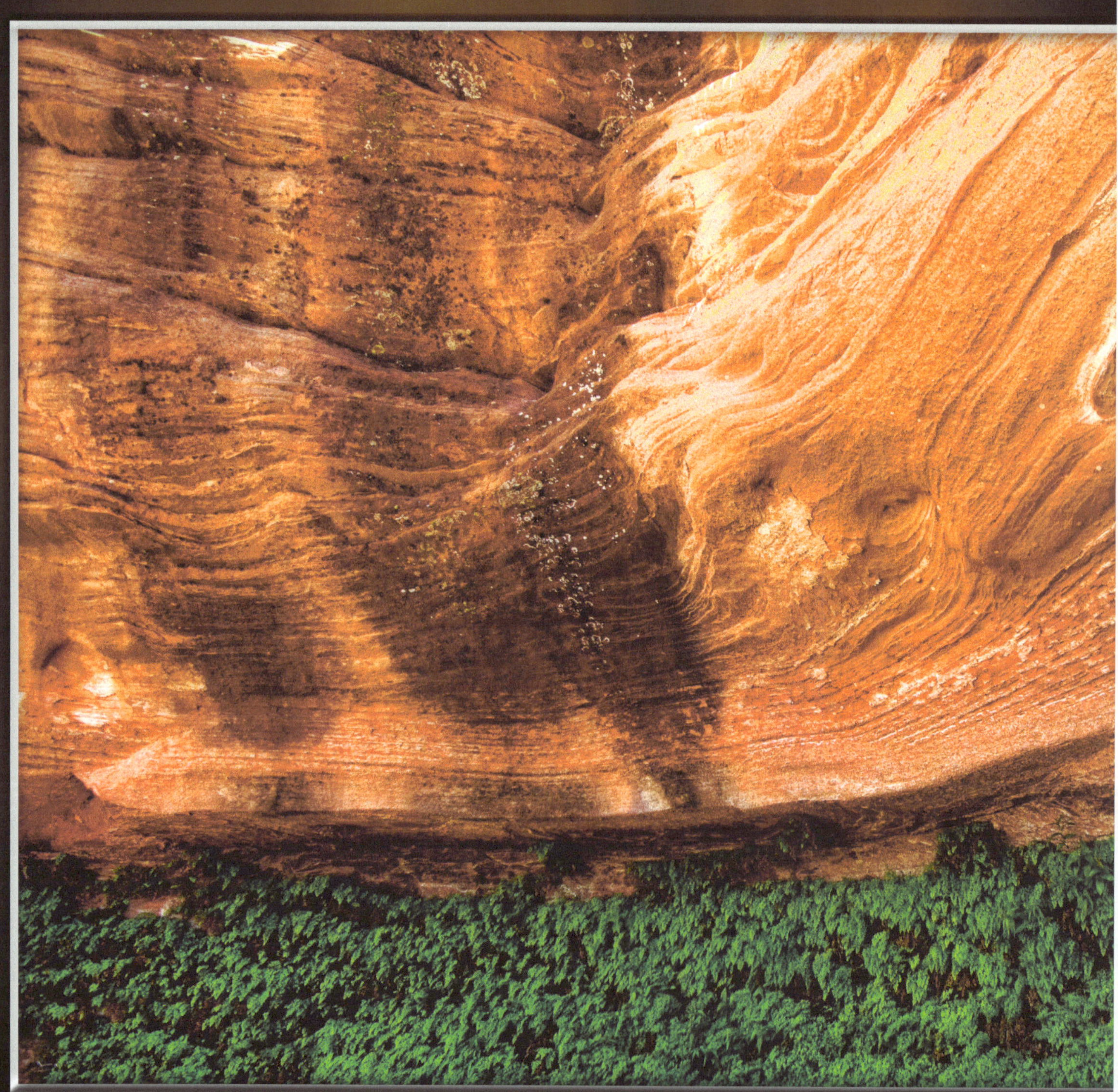

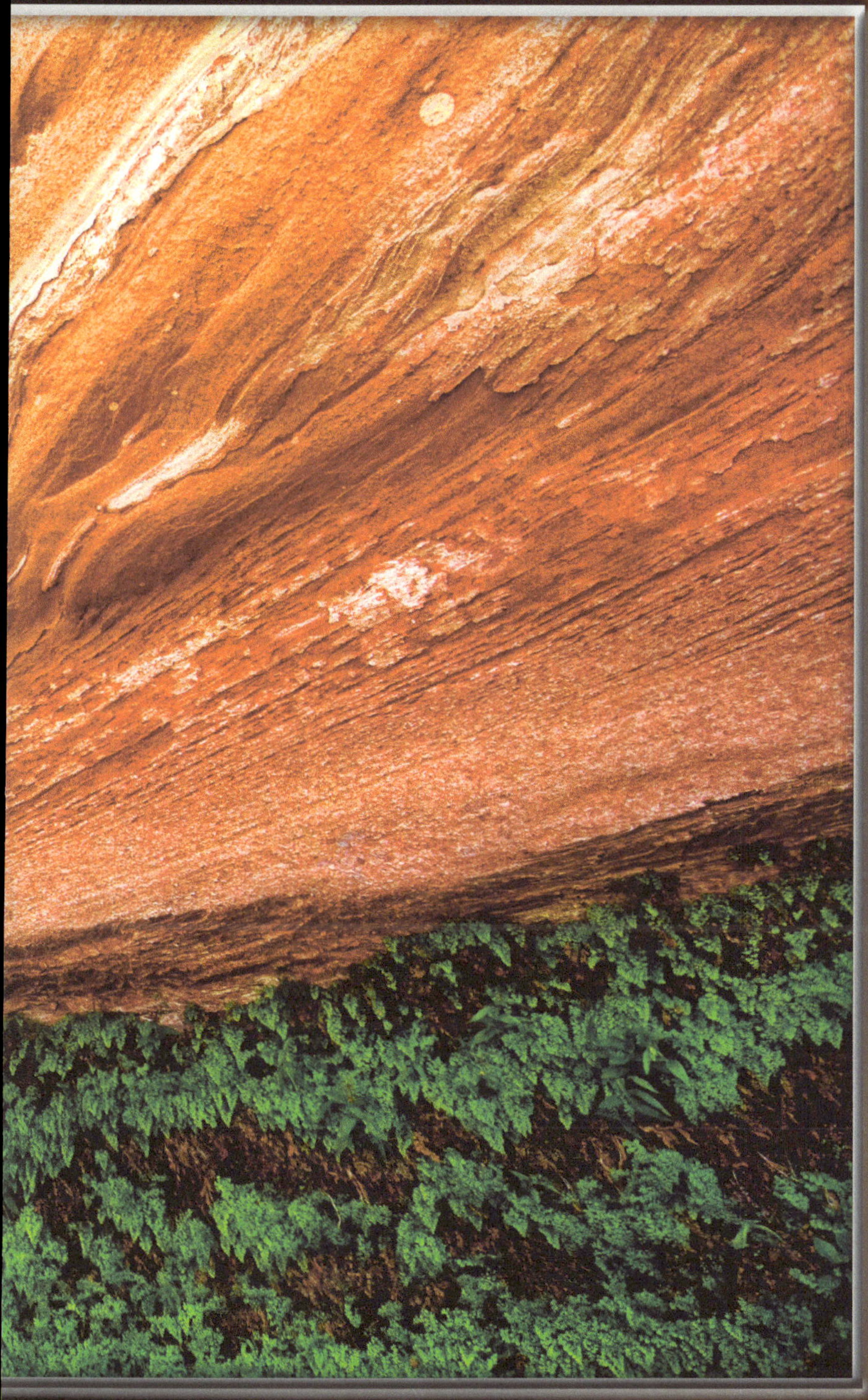

Humble Magistone

Ever wonder why the rocks are smiling?
You will never know if you don't stop to listen.

From dust, this sandstone came, and to dust it will return. But right now, it's nurturing life... and smiling.

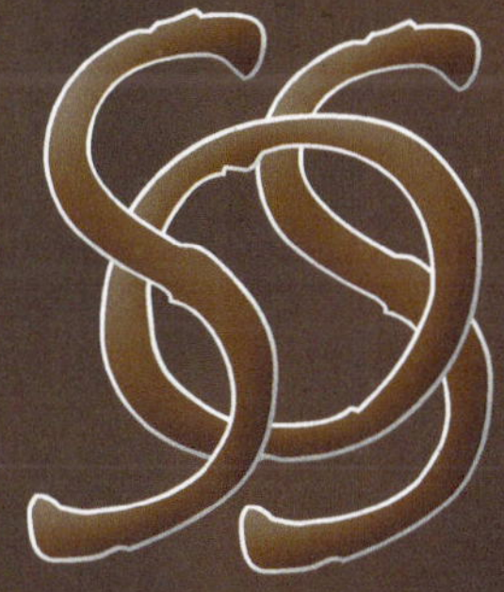

Sound of Silence

Grand Staircase- Escalante National Monument

Southern Utah

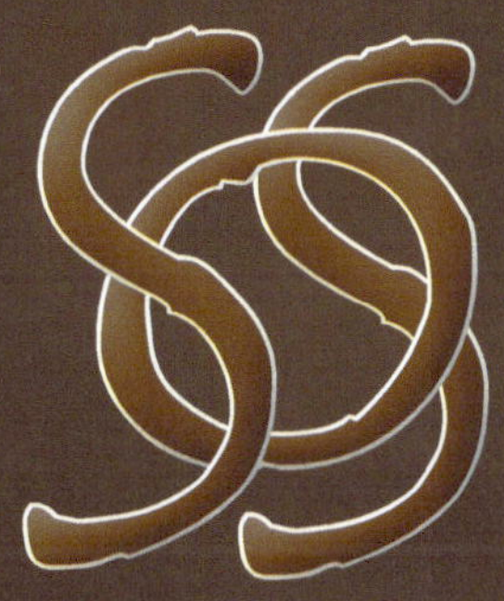

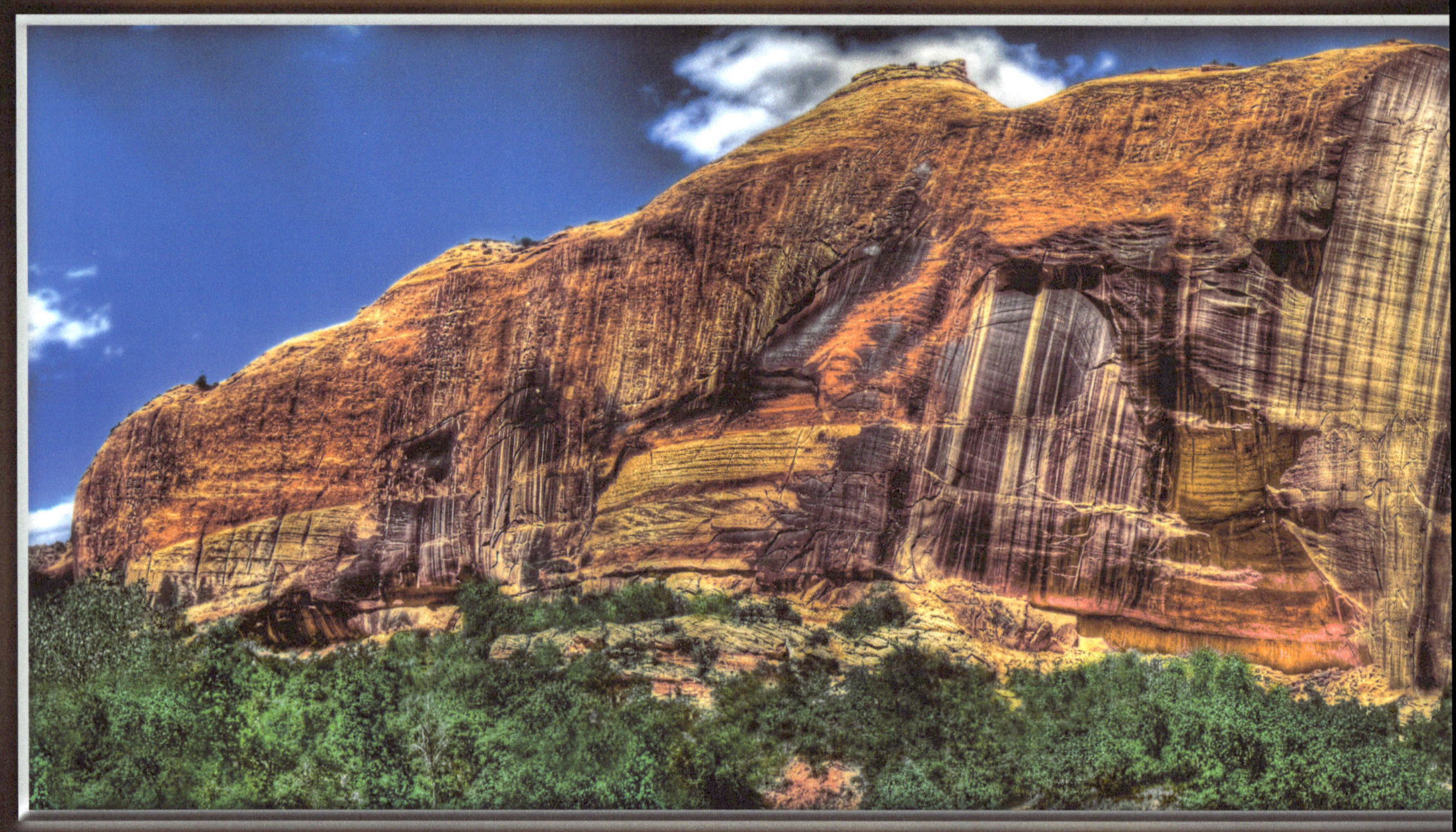

Sanctuary

Inside these walls is sanctuary.
A reprieve from what awaits outside.
In the desert, it is shelter from sun and sand.
Some days I need shelter from myself
and then find sanctuary in fellowship.

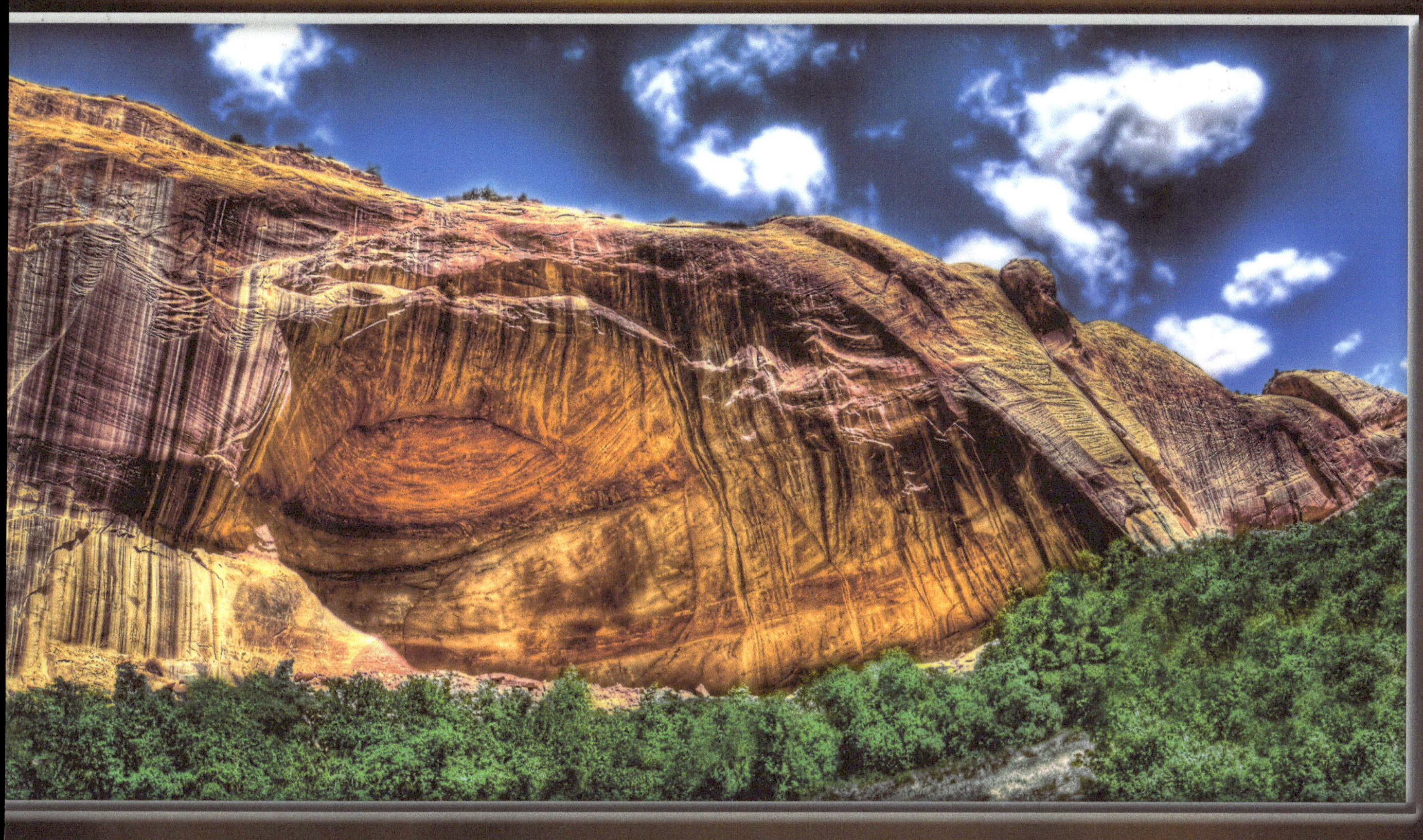

Me, Myself, and now?

My spines are long, their points sharp.
Come close and you may bleed.
Yet, how vulnerable these tender petals feel,
pushed forth, seeking new life.

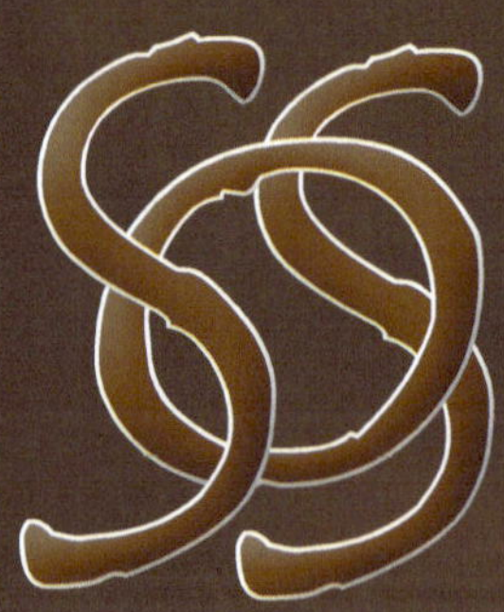

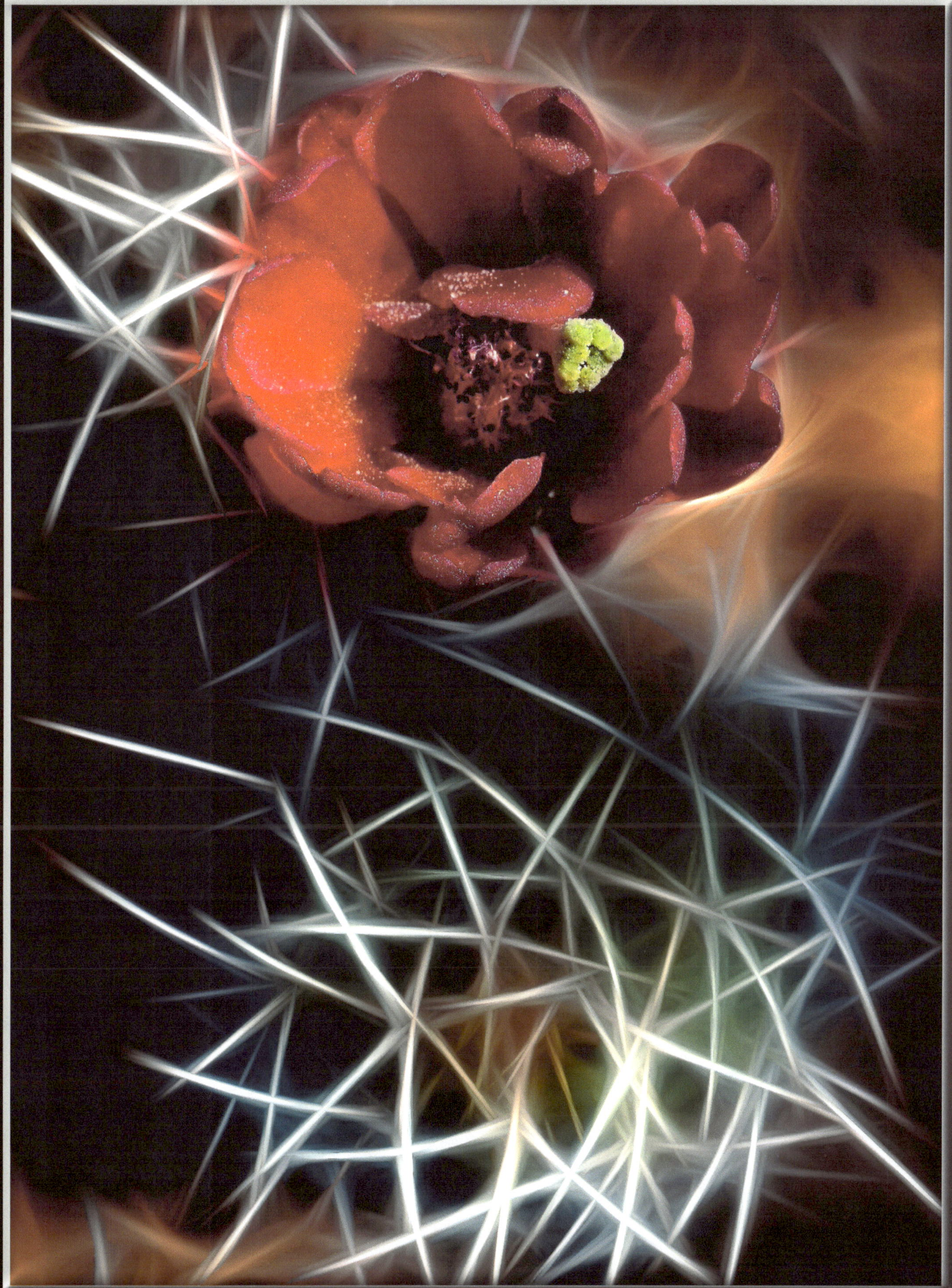

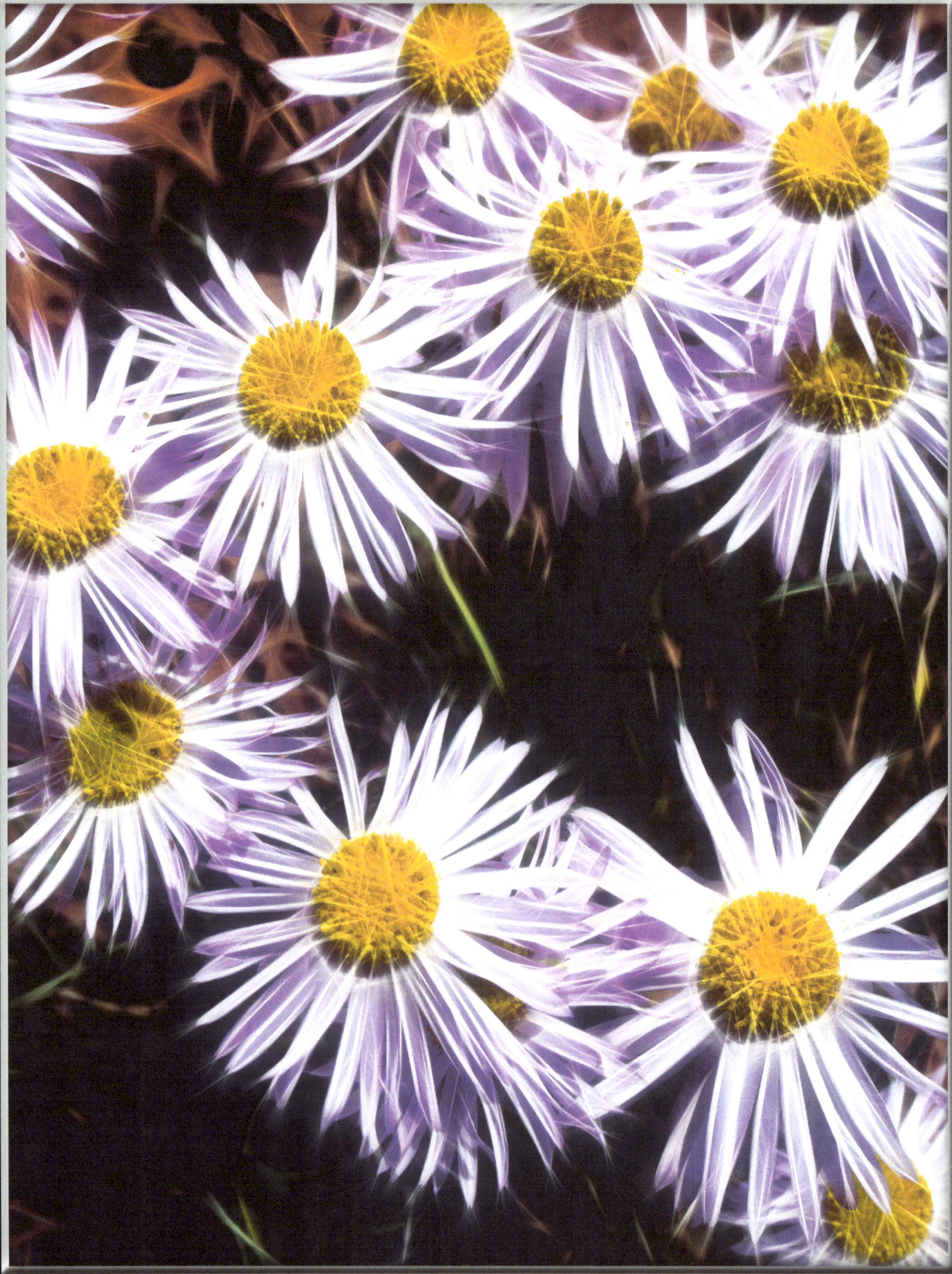

As Above, So Below

Are desert flowers more beautiful

then their rain forest or

rose garden cousins?

Maybe not.

But only seekers find flowers here.

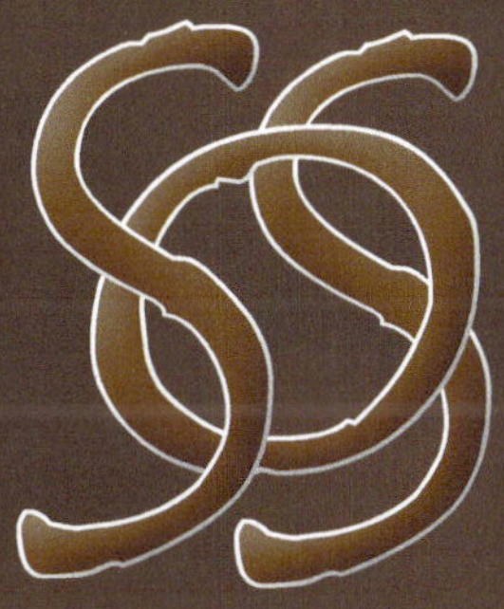

Empty Vessels Get Filled the Most.

Stop here - sit awhile.

Listen to her song.

Hear the stories she tells.

If you are empty,

She will fill you.

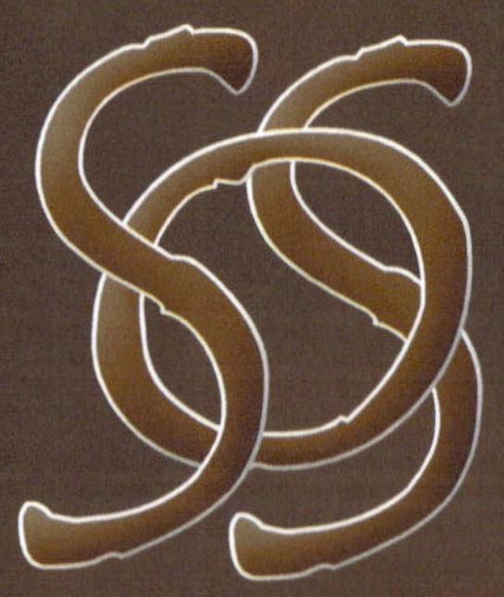

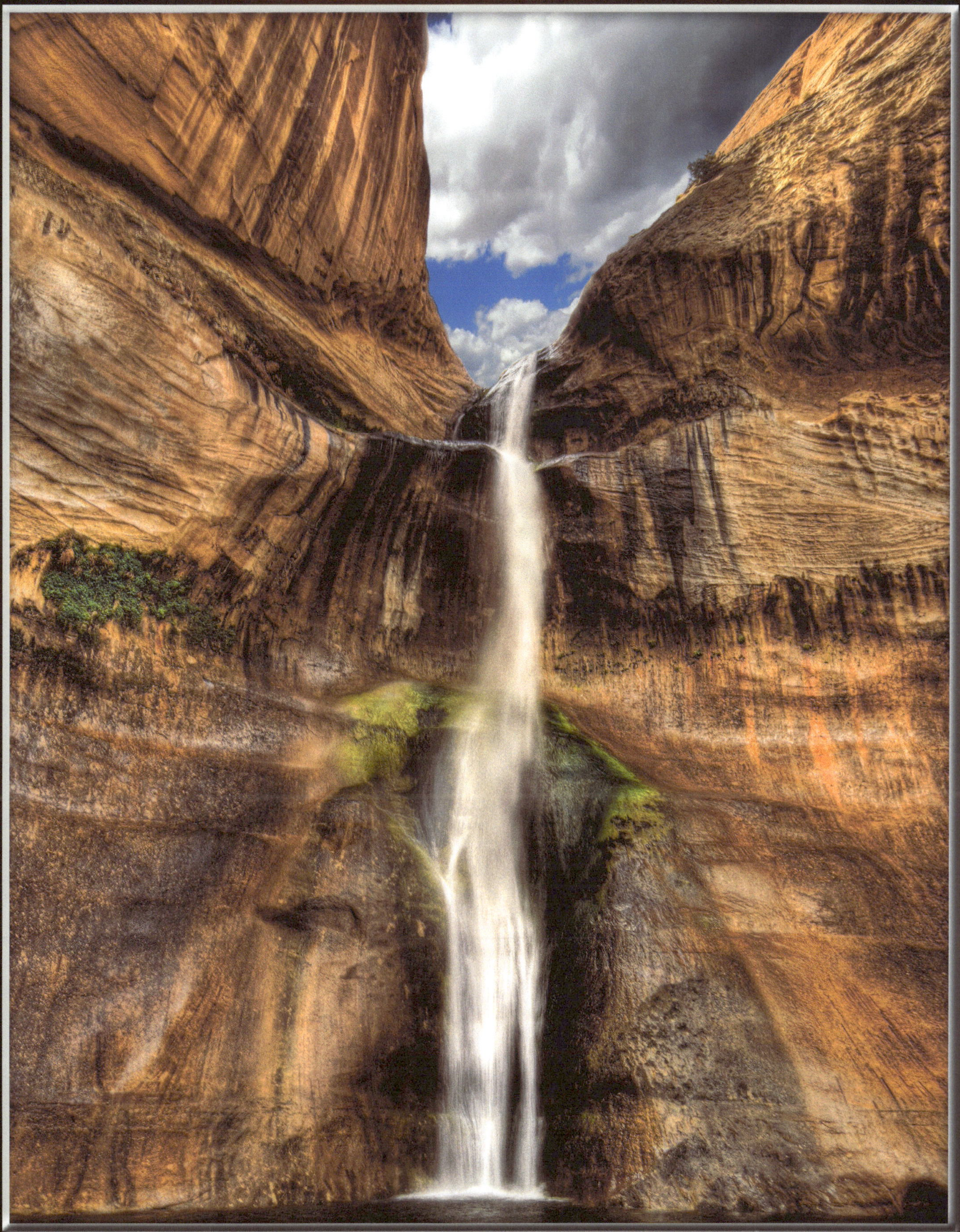

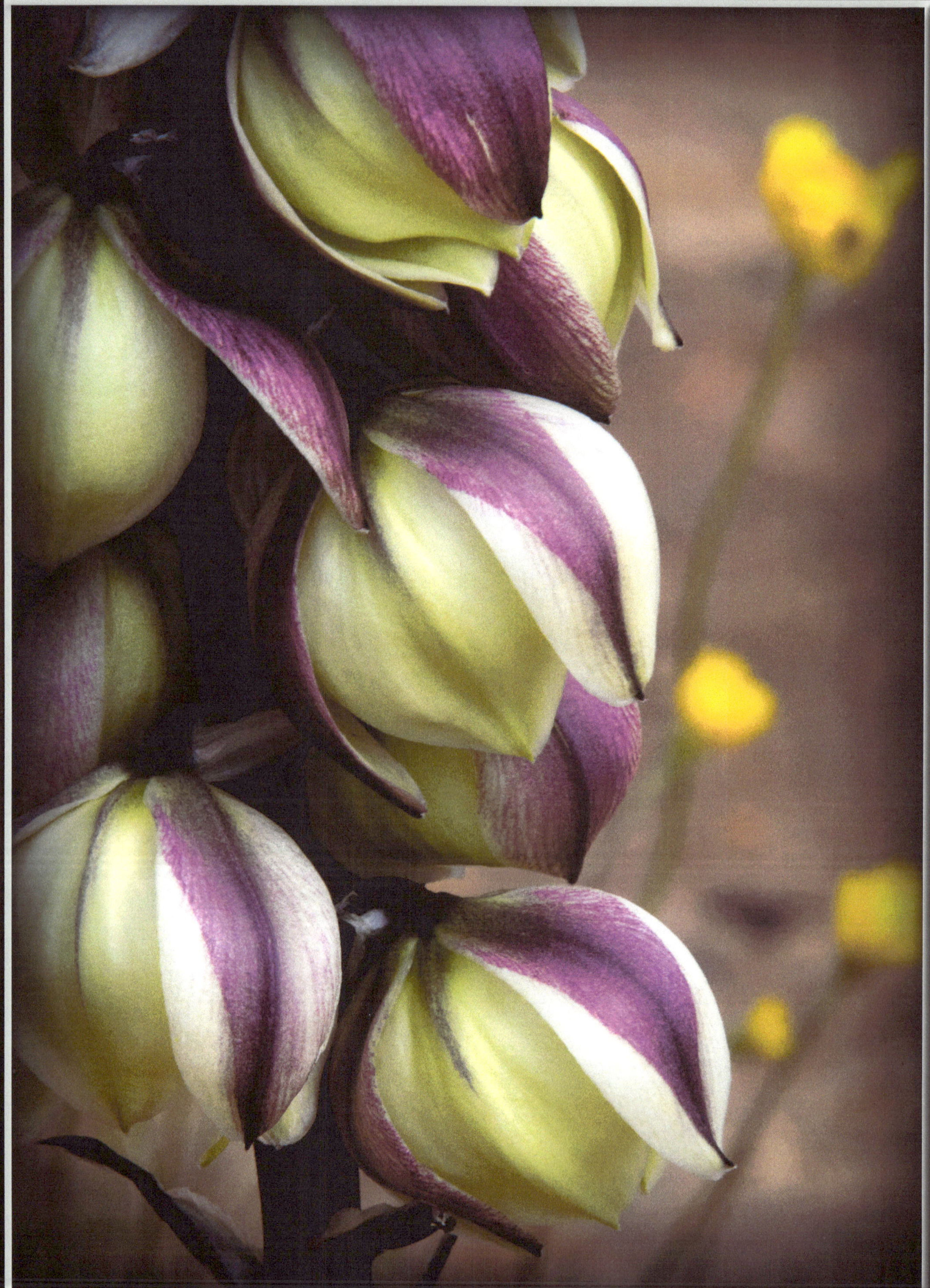

Opening

Some people become like
plants in the desert.
Covered with hard spines
and thorns for protection.
But in the right conditions,
they WILL begin to flower.

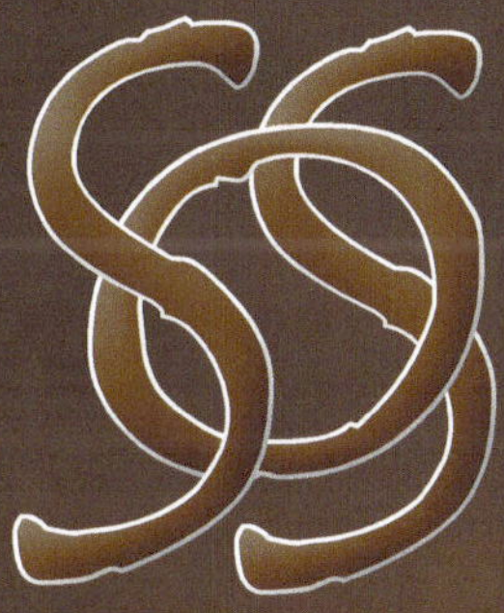

For Freedom

Safe within friendly walls...
Blossoms begin to outnumber
thorns inside troubled hearts.
It's good practice!
True freedom from bondage
comes from offering yourself
naked on the altar of forgiveness.

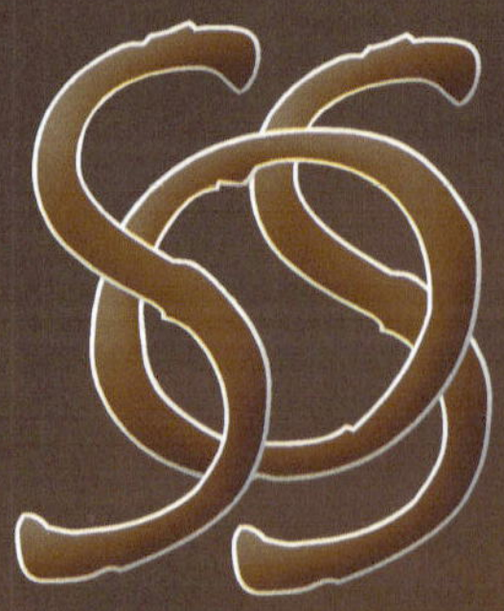

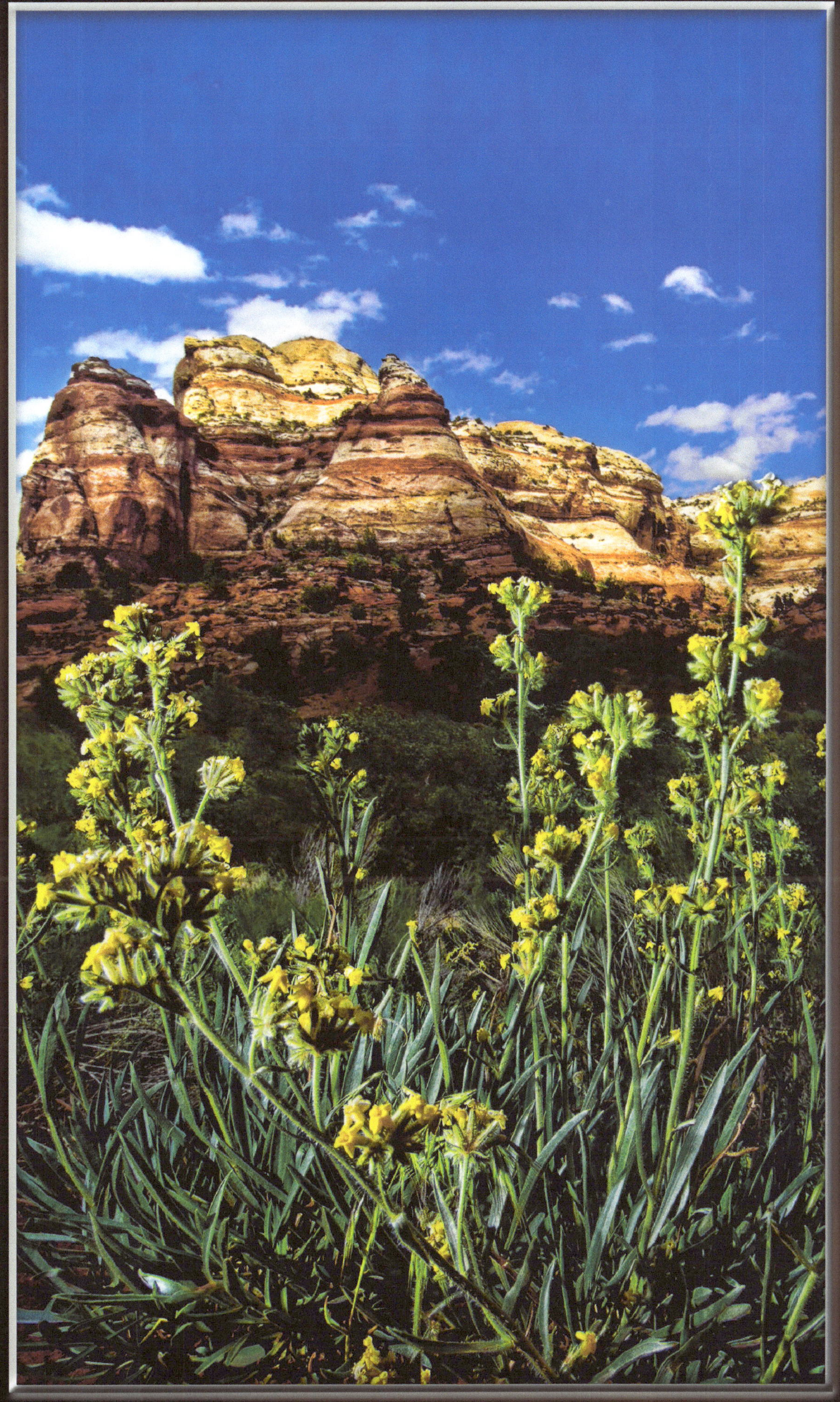

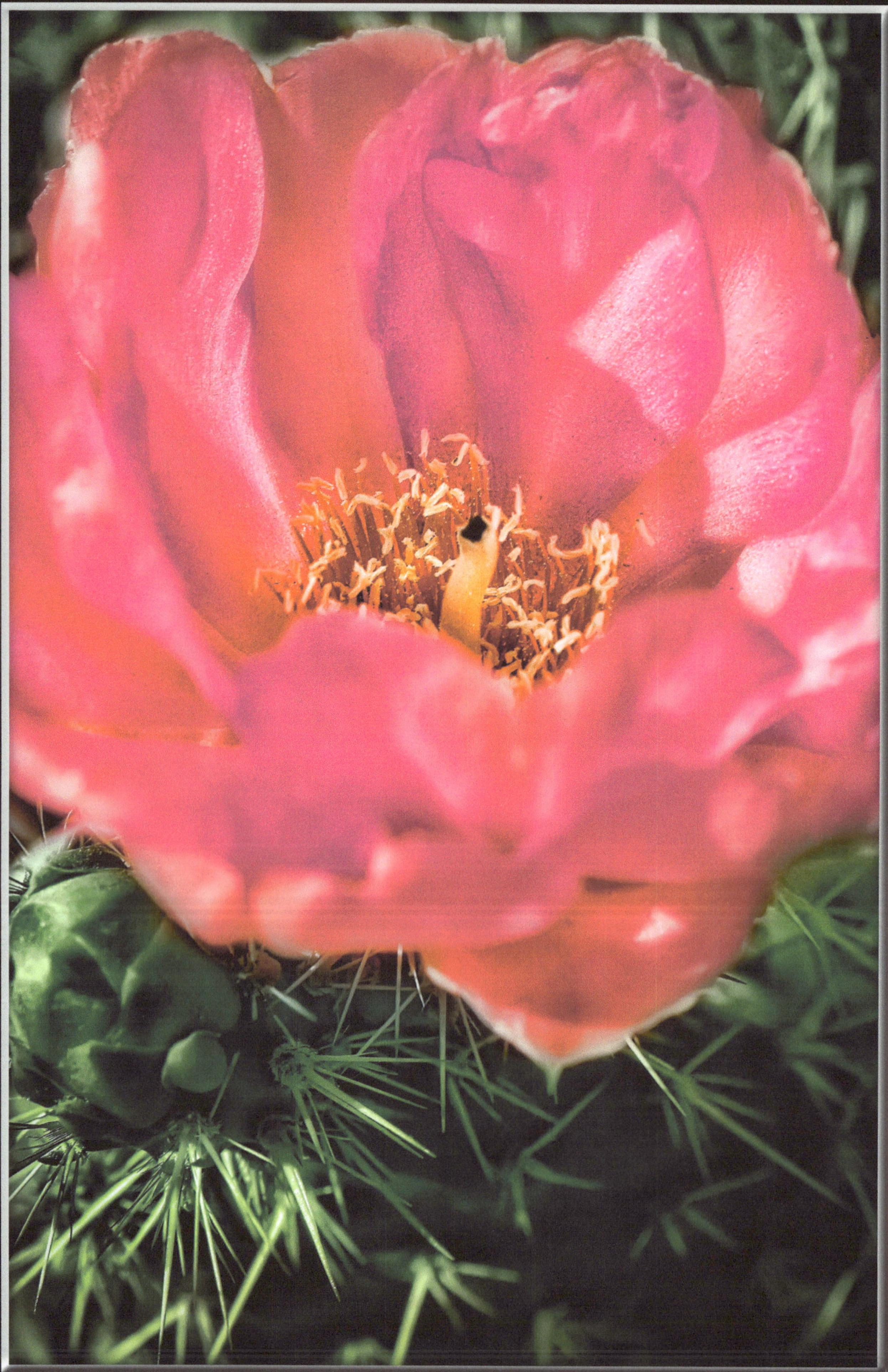

Hope

Tender pink petals fearlessly displayed
in a thousand square miles of desert.
This is what hope looks like!

There are many types of dying.
In some, your heart stops beating.
In the worst, it stops believing.

I had to loose all hope
before it could find me again...

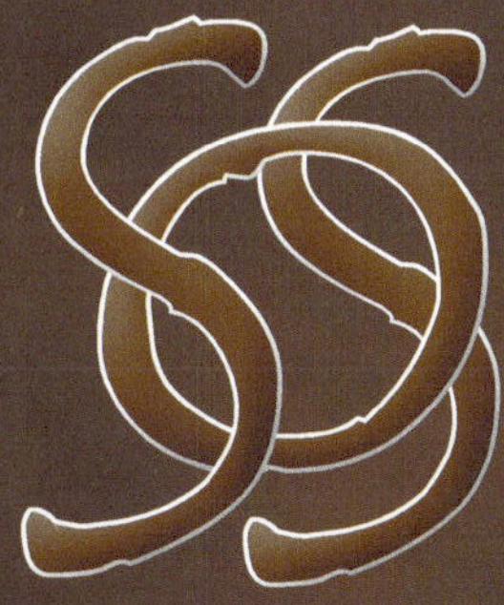

My Journey

In the Fall of 2010, I was told that in no uncertain terms, I was going to die... and soon. I had reached that place of absolute hopelessness that only someone whose body is shutting down from alcoholism, can understand. I was bloated with liquids that my damaged kidneys could not process, and in agony from a swollen liver. I had reached the "jumping off place." An endless cycle of DT's, seizures, and vomiting. If I continued to drink, I would die. And if I quit (without medical help), I would die. On October 31, 2010, I checked myself into a medical detox facility called Valley Hope, the only man-made place I consider truly hallowed ground.

So began my odyssey of recovery and My Journey for the Sound of Silence.

Three months later, my roommate and best friend, after three days of not drinking, had a massive withdrawal seizure in my arms. "Puppet" died at age 33 on February 3, 2011, after five days in the hospital.

Another three months later, six months after that life choosing Halloween night at Valley Hope, I set out in my old pick-up truck for the deserts of the Four Corners area. (I might add that five mountain passes later, I dubbed my truck "Bad- Ass George," for his unflagging perseverance.)

For more than 25 years, I had dreamed of doing a photo trek through the desert Southwest and I finally had the courage to do so. I was looking for something. To be honest, I did not find it while I was there. I think those days and nights with just myself and a tent prepared the soil for new growth. I know now that quitting drinking was only a step. I was soul-sick, and those few moments wrapped in the Sound of Silence were a poultice for the broken parts of me.

I returned home to the trials of work and school, love and loss. Twenty-four days later, another close friend died. His body shut down due to drinking. Martin died June 24, 2011 at age 34, leaving two beautiful daughters in the care of his parents. Every day, I wonder why I am alive and they are not. I honestly do not know and probably never will. It is what it is.

And so the odyssey continues. After nearly 30 years of taking photos, I am having my own gallery shows. One year, one month and 10 days since I chose life, I opened my Sound Of Silence mixed media show on December 9, 2011. Celebrating the one year anniversary of my return from the desert, I opened Sound of Silence II, along with the release of this book on June 15, 2012.

I continue to make unique lamps, screens and fountains from the images I discovered on that trip. It is still hard to believe that not very long ago I couldn't hold a camera, let alone drive across the country. Each and every day, I am grateful for that day's reprieve and my chance for a new life.

The idea that was spawned many years ago has a whole new and humbling meaning for me. For when I am alone in silence, I clearly hear the boisterous laughter of Matt and Jeff, who laughed more loudly and often than anyone else I have ever known.

To Mom

I will never really know what it took to raise three kids alone, nor can I truly grasp the moments of doubt, fear or heartache you have endured. The sacrifices, the burdens shouldered, the loneliness, the strength, the bravery, the endurance. I remember being 27 years old when I first realized you were afraid of mice. I was really shocked. How can this be? We lived in the house in Victoria with all the mice in the walls, and I never knew this. Mom wasn't afraid of anything. She did what needed to be done.

I grew up a lot that day, realizing that you are a person with all the hopes, dreams, fears and all the emotions we all have, but because you were Mom, you didn't show them. You had to be strong. You had to make the best of it. While I wish you hadn't had to carry all those burdens alone, I am truly glad you did. I know at times, I have made you sad and other times, you have feared terribly for me. I am in a good place now, and everything that brought me here is from you. Everything good in me I can attribute directly to you: determination, hard work, a genuine caring for others, a passion for creative thinking and creative doing, a love of reading, problem solving and so much more.

Around the same time, I realized the most important thing I know about you. I was talking fondly about our long, hot Kansas road trips, in an old car without AC. I would passionately describe my new theories and ideas. During one such trip, I told you that all world religions were founded on the same principles but were never practiced according to those principles. Because they have to be practiced by man, he is filled with desires that go against those principles. Oh, how proud I was of this idea; I talked about it for hours, as you quietly listened and commented.

Many years later, I learned you were really upset about that talk. You feared for me when I spoke of the religions I had read about. As a stout Catholic at heart, you were frightened that I was endangering my soul. You feared you had made a mistake, encouraging my reading and thinking about such thoughts, especially so young. But you never let on. Not for one second did I feel anything but encouragement and interest. At first, when I learned how it upset you, I was hurt and felt betrayed. The one person whom I could always bounce my ideas off of didn't like them, or at least understand them. Rather arrogant, I know.

Thankfully, that lasted but a moment. Then, I realized the truth. I had the best Mother in the whole world. She never demanded I think as she did, she encouraged my growth and learning to become my own self, even if it scared her. Even now, the power of that act of selfless love brings tears to my eyes. And Mom, I know you can't be Mom and not worry about your kids. But please know you did the right thing, and you did it well. -For only seekers find flowers here!

"Mother is the word for God on the lips and hearts of little children."
- William Thackery
In her arms, I first knew comfort. From her voice, I first learned peace.
From her heart, I learned the depths of love.

I love you, Mom!

www.ingramcontent.com/pod-product-compliance
Lightning Source LLC
LaVergne TN
LVHW070147110826
845147LV00002B/337
* 9 7 8 0 9 8 5 9 9 3 9 0 0 *